OUTSMARTING GOLIATH: HOW TO ACHIEVE EQUAL FOOTING WITH COMPANIES THAT ARE BIGGER, RICHER, OLDER, AND BETTER KNOWN

by Debra Koontz Traverso

"**This book has it all**—commonsense ideas you can use right now, technology tips for the future, and an easy-to-read, motivating style. *Outsmarting Goliath* is **a must-read for every small business owner who doesn't want to stay small**."

> DON TAYLOR
> President and CEO, Data Staar Communications
> Coauthor of *Up Against the Wal-Marts*

"In *Outsmarting Goliath,* Debra Koontz Traverso gives small businesses far more than a slingshot. She gives them a lush arsenal of lethal marketing weapons and insights that they can use to defeat the giants and beautify their own bottom lines. **Her book is informative, readable, and filled with the kind of wisdom that actually gives the Davids of the world just the armament they need against the Goliaths.** If I were a Goliath, this book would make me quake in my boots."

> JAY CONRAD LEVINSON
> Author of the best-selling Guerrilla Marketing book series

Outsmarting Goliath

BLOOMBERG SMALL BUSINESS

Debra Koontz Traverso

Outsmarting Goliath

HOW TO ACHIEVE EQUAL FOOTING WITH COMPANIES THAT ARE BIGGER, RICHER, OLDER, AND BETTER KNOWN

BLOOMBERG PRESS

PRINCETON

This publication contains the author's opinions and is designed to provide accurate and authoritative information. It is sold with the understanding that the author, publisher, and Bloomberg L.P. are not engaged in rendering legal, accounting, investment-planning, or other professional advice. The reader should seek the services of a qualified professional for such advice; the author, publisher, and Bloomberg L.P. cannot be held responsible for any loss incurred as a result of specific investments or planning decisions made by the reader.

First edition published 2000

1 3 5 7 9 10 8 6 4 2

Library of Congress Cataloging-in-Publication Data
Koontz Traverso, Debra.
Outsmarting Goliath: how to achieve equal footing with companies that are bigger, richer, older, and better known / Debra Koontz Traverso.
    p.   cm.
Includes index.
ISBN 1-57660-031-9
1. Small business - - Management. 2. Competition. I. Title.

HD62.7.K668   2000
658.02'2--dc21   99-054588

EDITED BY
Jared Kieling

BOOK DESIGN BY
Don Morris Design

To my parents, Clair and Mary Koontz, for always encouraging me to work hard, do what I love, and create a life with few regrets so that it will be worth remembering when I am old; and to my son, Matthew, for making each day of my life worth living

ACKNOWLEDGMENTS

THIS BOOK IS THE RESULT OF YEARS OF SUCCESS, EXPERIENCE, frustration, and tremendous heartache—for both myself and the hundreds of small business owners I have met, consulted with, listened to, and cheered on. It pleases me that for most of them, I can say, "I knew them when."

I want to thank all the people quoted in this book who endured hours of sharing war stories, walking down memory lane, answering questions, and responding to my endless requests to "be a bit more specific."

No writer can work for very long without taking breaks. Fortunately, it's possible to return to the work fully refreshed when those breaks are filled with stimulation, encouragement, and support from colleagues, friends, and family like these: Kathy Belcher, Denise Crouse, Debbie Duncan, David Edelman, Rochelle Jones, Mary Koontz, Dottie McAdams, Jim Morrison, Charles Boston, Kerry Stanley, Ginny Sulcer, Lee Turner, and Richard Wilkins.

When the going gets tough, the writer's block sets in, and the latest chapter is forever lost to Cyberland, every writer should have an irreplaceable friend and business partner like Beth Mende Conny. Thanks, Beth.

Much thanks also to my agent team, Mike and Pat Snell, for giving me great advice and counsel on this and every book I've ever proposed.

And finally, no book can be a success without the experts to position it and guide its development. This expertise came from the professionals at Bloomberg Press. Many thanks for the best writing experience I've ever had to my editor, Jared Kieling, and former editor, Jacqueline Murphy. Thanks to Barbara Diez for continually shuffling my e-mail in the right direction, and to Melissa Hafner, Susan Stawicki, Maris Williams, Christina Palumbo, Tracy Tait, and Bloomberg's marketing team.

Introduction

SINCE LEAVING A MANAGERIAL PUBLIC RELATIONS
position with a Goliath more than ten years ago to
start my own management consulting firm, I have
been through a few incarnations—first as owner of
a small business, then as a crisis management
adviser to other Goliaths, and now as a writer,
trainer, speaker, and consultant.

Despite the changes in my relationship with the
Goliaths—first for them, then against them, then
with them, and now independent of them—the
questions I get from small business owners have
been variations of one theme: How can I compete
with the big guys? For them—and for you—I have
put together this book full of tactics that small
business owners can use to outsmart their bigger,
richer, older, and better-known competition; tactics
that can land them assignments and sales from
larger organizations. Predominantly, the tips center
on the attitude, character, creativity, delivery,

demeanor, ingenuity, identity, positioning, and stability of the business, its owner, and its employees.

From this book you will learn where you are now, where you need to be, what tactics and changes can help you get there, and what to do when you have arrived. You must provide the diligence; this book will serve as the insight. This insight comes from my years in the trenches. For almost ten years, I operated a successful small business offering crisis management expertise, and—although it consisted of just my partner and me and a few part-time associates—we landed impressive contracts with organizations such as UPS, NASA, Battelle Corp., Schlumberger Ltd., Jet Propulsion Laboratory, and scores of utilities, many with more than 5,000 employees. Sometimes we beat larger competitors for the contracts. At other times, our presentation and reputation alone awarded us contracts without any competitors in the running.

My work has always involved learning many valuable little (and big) company secrets in order to carry out my assignments. Companies had to trust me and treat me as one of their own for me to be able to consult effectively with them—a trust that I will always honor. As a result, I got to see their insides and how they function. I was able to compete *against* Goliaths to win major contracts *with* Goliaths. I also got close enough to see how these companies can trip themselves. I learned a valuable lesson in my management work: it's only from the very top or the very bottom that you can learn how a company of any size works. Any level in between offers only a small and tainted view of the bigger picture. Thus, simply being a small business does give you a competitive edge. This book will tell you how to use it.

All of the characters and scenarios in this book are real; however, often the names have been changed to protect anonymity and to honor my allegiance to my resources. After all, I want to practice what I preach in this book. Allegiance—to your customers, partners, associates, and confidants—is one of the most powerful tactics you will be able to use to outsmart your bigger, older, richer, and better-known competition. Many other tactics are identified herein. So grab a cup of coffee, and let's get started on outsmarting the Goliaths in your industry.

CHAPTER 1

Crafting the Right Image

ASSESS YOUR CURRENT IMAGE

PROFILING YOUR CLIENTS' PERCEPTION OF YOUR BUSINESS

YOU HAVE CAPITAL, A SOLID BUSINESS PLAN, a good product or service at the right price—along with the competence to produce and deliver it, a sizable potential market, and a well-equipped office. What you don't have: customers. Your market seems to gravitate toward the bigger or more established companies—the dominators in your industry. You begin to wonder: Can you compete? Can you make it? Can you win clients, contracts, and market share away from the corporate behemoths?

The answers are yes, yes, and yes. Like David in the biblical account of the young boy who slew the giant Goliath, you can outsmart your bigger and well-established competition. David had a slingshot and five stones to help him. You have this book and the trait necessary to make it happen: determination.

The Small Business Edge

YOU DON'T HAVE TO HAVE AN ACRONYM FOR A COM- pany name to be a success, and you don't have to be in the *Fortune* 500 to be competitive in the marketplace. Outsmarting the competition doesn't always mean breaking them, or outpacing them, or even giving them a run for their money. Instead, as this book demonstrates, it can mean becoming a respected leader in your market in spite of their existence. While the big guys are throwing their weight around, it's possible for you to quietly thrive as an underdog. After all, being small has its benefits. It's easier to manage your business, respond to your customers, and react to market fluctuations when you're not bogged down by corporate weight.

The problem is that in this "big is best" world of corporate America you must appear to be sizable, reliable, successful, and proven if you want to win customers. So how can you compete if you appear to be small, new, untested, and untried? The answer is not better computer equipment, more start-up capital, and a larger budget. Those may help, but they'll also increase your debt. The answer is changing your image to one that says *knowledgeable, experienced, reliable,* and *well established.*

The Image You Present

THE APPROPRIATE CORPORATE IMAGE IS ONE OF THE MOST valuable assets a company has for winning customers, especially for a home-based or small business. A good image will enable you to attract customers and investors, expand operations, and survive economic downturns. A bad image is a costly liability, even if you're capable of doing the job.

This chapter is about the image of your business that you create in the minds of your potential customers. Excellence peddlers would tell you that all you need to succeed is a commitment to customer service, while business schools would credit good management as the road to success. Sure, it's both of these things and more, but overriding these ideals is the *image* in your prospects' minds of whether or not you possess or strive for the ideals.

I'm not suggesting the classic start-up scam in which you try to come off as something you are not. And I'm not suggesting you work to the brink of physical, emotional, and spiritual exhaustion. I'm referring more to an enhancement of what you already do on a daily basis. For example, today it's possible to run an international conglomerate from an apartment. Our society relishes the freedom to do that. But the same members of our society who love that freedom would simultaneously scoff at an international conglomerate being located in Apartment 8C at 121 Magnolia Blossom

Drive. So, for example, the simple enhancement this entrepreneur should make to stop tripping himself is to move his office or rent a mailbox at an impressive-sounding address. Dishonest? No. Smart image crafting.

Image Crafting

LET'S USE AN ANALOGY THAT'S EASY TO UNDERSTAND: THE typical résumé—something we've all prepared during our professional lives. In the same way we practice word crafting on our résumés to make our experience sound the best that it can, we have to practice image crafting in our business to make it sound and look the best that it can. For example, let's say that in your former job you "suggested changes for the distribution center that saved time and eliminated redundancy." Do you say that on your résumé? Yes, if it's true. But you don't use those words. Instead, you give the same honest presentation using a little word crafting: "Initiated improvements at the distribution center, increasing productivity by 145 percent." It's the same thing, but the latter creates a better impression of your work and a measurement of your achievement.

On that same résumé, you strive to express that you are enough of a maverick to run with any project independently, but that you are a team player when need arises. Likewise in your work, whether you're self-employed, running a small business, or part of a team building a start-up, your dichotomous task is to convince the world that you are big enough to be knowledgeable, experienced, reliable, and well established but still small enough to care.

Understanding Image

IMAGE IS MORE THAN WHAT YOU SAY YOU ARE. IT'S MORE THAN your statements to the world of what your company does. All the facets of your business have positive or negative effects on your company's reputation. A company's image is composed of all planned and unplanned verbal, visual, and other sensory elements that emanate from you and

Five Factors Controlling the Company Image

YOUR BUSINESS—like all businesses—projects an image of some sort whether you are aware of it or not. Awareness is your first step toward having control. Let's look at five factors that influence your image:

1 Your company logistics. Logistics include your industry, your size and structure, the number of employees you have, your location, how your store or office looks and sounds, the products or services you provide, and how much you interact with the community and your clients. Without even knowing you, people have a preconceived impression of your business. This preconception, if favorable, works to a small business owner's advantage, because people have a better idea of what they might encounter through their patronage. When companies become chain operations, their scope changes and their product line or list of services begins to shift; customers are no longer sure what to expect. Often people will stick with the reliable and the familiar, provided the smaller company makes it worth their while by keeping all other factors—such as customer service, price, and quality—equal to or better than those of the growing competition.

2 Your uniqueness and how you differentiate yourself from the competition. In item one, I said that being consistent and fulfilling customers' preconceived notions was good, and now I'm saying you have to be unique. How can you do both? Let's say you run a bookstore. People have an idea of what to expect from a bookstore, and you shouldn't let them down. They want to find a selection of books categorized under subject headings in a brightly lit store. And nowadays, they might also expect a place to sit down and have a cup of coffee. What they won't expect but will be pleased to discover is a place to hang their coats and stash their bags so their hands are free to leaf through potential purchases. They might not expect access to the Internet to look up reviews of a book. (Even if you have to log onto Amazon.com so that you can provide them with reviews, they're still likely to buy the book from your store because your books are available and the shipping cost at Amazon.com often takes a big bite out of the discount they offer.) And customers might not expect to find a kids' club that awards a prize (not a book) to any child who purchases and reads a certain number of books in a given time.

3 Your company's scope and depth. This is another area in which a small business can take advantage of its size. Big and diverse can become big and diffuse—the more varied a large business's activities, the more varied the messages it sends out. Multiple claims and promotions work against a cohesive message, making it confusing for consumers to develop an impression of a company. Their own confusion is transferred to the company; thus, the impression is that the company is so large that confusion and perhaps even chaos must reign there. In contrast, a small business can speak in one voice, giving one message, one direction, one theme. Communications tend to appear more consistent.

4 Your communications efforts. Being seen and being remembered are two important goals for any business. If you're a new business, you need to conduct a strong and extensive communications effort to educate the public about your existence and availability. Because you are a smaller business on a tight budget, you'll have to communicate in many nontraditional ways and do it again and again.

5 Service. Service is probably your best edge over the competition, even more so than price. You are closer to your customers than most larger companies can get. You can also more easily bend, break, and invent policy to satisfy your customer. Would you want to buy a computer at a lower price if you knew the big discounter's customer telephone service line averaged a waiting time of an hour or more? Most people will pay a little more to ensure they are purchasing from a company that is readily available—if they are made aware of the difference.

every aspect of your company and leave an impression on customers or prospects. Yes, this means that if customers trip on the carpet coming in your door or notice musty odors, those negative experiences will affect your image, too.

Conduct an Image Assessment

YOU MAY BE THE BEST IN YOUR FIELD OR HAVE THE BEST product on the market. But if your market audience has a perception different from that reality, then that perception is where you need to direct your image development.

Determine what your customers' perception is of your company and whether your current image is helping or stifling your growth and sales. Honest answers to the following questions will get you started. Are you:

◆ **Accessible?**
   —How easy is it to buy from you? For example, if you sell products on the Internet, can you take credit cards?
   —Do you maintain local inventory?
   —What lead times are required?
   —Do you offer a live answering service?
   —Do you have convenient hours?
   —Do you have a toll-free number?
   —Do you offer free delivery?
   —Is parking available?
   —Are you easy to reach without having to cross a busy road?
   —Are you located with other high-traffic stores or offices?

◆ **Appealing?**
   —Are staff members dressed appropriately?
   —Are they positive, helpful, respectful?
   —Do they look customers in the eye and greet them pleasantly?
   —Do they show pride in working at your organization?
   —Is your store or office pleasant looking? Clean? Safe?
   —Does it smell welcoming, or is the aroma stale or strong?
   —Is it audibly friendly, or is it noisy, such as from clanging machinery or employees yelling from room to room?

—Do the decorations and office furniture support the pre-sentation of the work that you do?

—Is your store or office organized or cluttered?

—Are products presented attractively?

—Are all visual and verbal messages emanating from your office of a professional nature?

◆ **Customer-focused?**

—Do you know who your customers are?

—Have you profiled them?

—How old are they?

—Where do they live?

—How much money do they make?

—What are their interests?

—What do they need?

—What do they want?

—What kinds of jobs do they have?

—What kinds of media do they use?

—Do you solicit and address complaints?

—Does your marketing material describe customer benefits rather than seller's features?

—Do you know the best ways to reach your customers? To appeal to them? To persuade them?

◆ **Dependable?**

—Can you deliver on time?

—Can you change delivery to accommodate clients?

—Do you offer guarantees?

—Do you honor them?

—Are all things dependably consistent when customers walk through the door, or are they unsure what to expect or where to find things or what your policy is this week?

—Do you consistently offer quality?

◆ **Priced competitively?**

—Are your products priced right?

—Do you offer quantity discounts?

—Do you offer payment plans and purchase incentives?

—Are repeat customers rewarded for their patronage?

◆ **Unique?**

—Do you conduct your services or sales differently?

—Can you solve problems that prospects have with current vendors?

—Is there something different about your business that appeals to prospects?

◆ **Visible?**

—Are you a good citizen?

—Are you involved in your community?

—Is your company mentioned in the local media or in trade publications?

—Do you attend industry conferences?

—Do you communicate consistent messages on a consistent schedule with your audience?

Image Improvement Plan

ONCE YOU CAN REALISTICALLY DESCRIBE YOUR IMAGE AS IT IS now, you can determine the best ways to change it into what you want it to be. Reading and marking up this book can give you a strategy for outsmarting your competition.

As you read through this book, keep two things in mind:

1 Be open to new ideas, to new ways of doing things. Creativity is generally rewarded in our society. Take the ideas presented in this book and adapt them. There is no right or wrong approach (provided it is ethically and legally sound) when it comes to operating a business. What's right for one company could result in disaster for another.

2 Don't overlook opportunities to improve your image. I have seen many business owners hurry past an unexpected opportunity to take their image to a higher level because it wasn't on their business plan. I won't embarrass any of them—I'll embarrass myself instead with a nonbusiness example of a time I overlooked the obvious. Once, while conducting training for a client in Green Bay, Wisconsin, it was necessary for me and a couple of my associates to arrive earlier than the employees, so we borrowed a key to the corporate headquarters. The next morning in the pouring rain, we were fumbling with the key, trying to figure out why it wouldn't work. Our goal was to open the door as fast as we could, because we were getting soaked. In our haste and our obliviousness to anything that didn't pertain to our goal, we didn't notice that a roll-up service door about twelve feet away was open. Our focus on the short-term goal of getting our key to work resulted in our overlooking an easy way out of the rain. Don't let this happen to your marketing endeavors.

PERFECT YOUR COMPANY'S NAME AND ADDRESS

CHOOSING A NAME AND LOCATION THAT BOLSTER YOUR IMAGE

HOW IMPORTANT IS YOUR NAME AND ADDRESS? WITHOUT A name for your company, you cannot achieve recall in your audience. Without recall, you will have no business. Without an address, customers won't know how to reach you. Need I say more?

Your Company's Name

THE VERY FIRST IMPRESSION OF YOUR COMPANY WILL BE derived from its name. The name is the quintessential element in your company's identity and image. You will want to open your company with the "perfect" name right from the start. But how do you determine the perfect name? This chapter will help.

I have long been a collector of business names, marveling at the plays on words and double meanings and descriptive terms people use in naming their companies. I can almost always tell what will work and what will not. That knowledge comes a little bit from my experience and research and a lot from gut instinct.

Unfortunately, current research confirms that naming a company is a highly subjective matter. Names have been created and changed through the years based upon a company's growth and diversification, cultural trends and fads, changes in social norms and outlooks, and development of technology. Starting in 1960, the New York Stock Exchange began keeping records of corporate name changes. Through the 1990s, it recorded well over 1,100 name changes among its common stock listings. *Advertising Age* reports that about 1,000 companies change their names each year. Clearly, naming a company is a strategic process requiring careful consideration. And little wonder. A name that is well chosen should last forever. When it has to be changed, the switch can lead to a loss of goodwill and recognition and, in some cases, to anonymity. Changing a company's name is also a very expensive process, involving legal fees and new stationery, packaging, and signs. Yet these expenses are dwarfed by the dollars required for advertising and marketing to reeducate the public. Nissan estimates that changing its name from Datsun took about three years and cost at least $30 million.

So why bother changing a name if it costs so much? The obvious answer is that the companies didn't select the right name the first time. The more studied answer is that companies that change their names feel the old names have become a liability and consider the change worth the expense. They cite one or more of the following reasons for a new name: accommodating change, announcing new directions or areas of corporate business, or inviting specific audiences to take a fresh look at what the company has become or is becoming.

In my opinion—and research supports this—a successful name will have three qualities: brevity, distinctiveness, and longevity. Take, for example, the name Humana. It's brief: a name of more than three syllables is too long and will be shortened by the public in ways you may not like. The name is distinctive: it can stand alone without other descriptive words, and it implies more warmth and dedication to "humanity" than the company's former name, Extendicare. And finally, Humana has longevity: it will not become outdated as the corporation diversifies or changes its core services. The change to the name Humana, by the way, resulted in an increase in market share and stock value. Other names that get an A-plus are Gymboree (short, sweet, descriptive,

and clearly connected with kids and fun) and Blockbuster
Video (does it matter whether the name applies to the products it sells or the store itself? Either way, the name suggests
volume and success).

SELECT THE PERFECT NAME

TO DETERMINE THE BEST NAME FOR YOUR BUSINESS, BENEFIT
from what other companies have learned the hard way:

◆ **Keep it short.** Almost two-thirds of corporate name
changes involve shortening the name; for example, dropping
such descriptors as "Manufacturing," "Glass," and "Steel."
This is not surprising, since many companies start by choosing a descriptive name, which in the short term saves communications dollars but proves too wordy as companies
diversify and become established. A short name may have
less communication content, but clearly it has more communication impact, since it will be easier to say and easier to
remember.

When my former partner and I opened our crisis management planning firm, he had been working with another
person for about six months as Technology and Management Planning Associates. As partners sometimes do, they
had decided to go separate ways due to differing goals for
the firm. Along I came, ready to launch a new business
and wanting the perfect name. I quickly discovered that
some of his clients were not prepared for a name change so
soon and might regard it as a sign we were a fly-by-night
organization.

Nevertheless I knew the firm had to change its name,
because it was too long. Fourteen syllables was cumbersome
and difficult for everyday usage. So, saddled with the need to
retain some of the old identity but knowing that we needed a
shorter name, my partner and I began a brainstorming ses-
sion. Our goal was to shorten the name in such a way that
the equity in the earlier name would be retained. We settled
on TECH*PLAN Associates. Lesson: Coin a brief, distinct
name from the start.

◆ **Avoid description, especially product description.** It's
been my experience that many name-makers demand

description. They want to "say what it is" so that people hearing it will know what the company does. Organizations that have gone through name changes, however, would disagree. They've learned that the purpose of a name is to designate, not describe, and that including your company's product in its name can constrain your company's image as it grows. Thus, Bausch and Lomb Optical became Bausch and Lomb. Why? Because the company had diversified, and because the public had long referred to it as Bausch and Lomb anyway.

Another well-known example of a company outgrowing its name is U.S. Steel Corp. In the 1980s, it changed its name to USX (the letter X was its symbol in stock trading). The new name was intended to portray a more diversified business portfolio; USX had become as much chemicals, engineering, consulting, transportation, oil, and gas as it was steel.

However, including a word of description in your name may serve you well until you've grown, especially if you *know* you will not diversify and you're *convinced* that the long name won't be shortened by your public in a manner you find works against you. Who could argue with snappy—and descriptive—names like Speedy Muffler King, Precision Tune, and Jiffy Lube? These names tell what the companies do *and* impart a benefit: the rapidity or exactness with which they service your vehicle. You have to use caution with description, however. I once saw a styling salon whose name, while clever, made me cringe: "We Curl Up and Dye." However, the First Light Café in San Francisco gets a thumbs-up for descriptive originality. Is there any doubt that this café opens early? Other favorites are a coffee bar called Grounds for Thought, a coffeehouse with music called Rhythm & Brews, a retired minister's bed-and-breakfast called Friar's Tuckaway, an Italian restaurant called The Great Impasta, and a car repair service called Engine Newity.

◆ **Drop geographic location.** When you grow beyond the original location, you will find a geographic name very limiting.

Eckerd Drugs of Florida realized its limiting name just before changing it to Eckerd Corp. Pittsburgh Plate Glass became PPG Industries, opting to drop both the geographic and the product descriptors, to avoid being confined by either category. US Airways used to be Allegheny Airlines. Before that change, more than 25 percent of travelers surveyed looked upon Allegheny as a regional airline, even though it was the sixth largest passenger airline in the United States. A good move, you think? Yes, but they limited themselves again when it came to expanding into the international marketplace. For example, U.S. Rubber changed to Uniroyal because company offices overseas were occasionally attacked by groups of anti-American demonstrators who believed that the company was part of the U.S. government.

◆ **Be distinctive.** High-tech industries need to learn this lesson. It has become very popular for computer firms, for example, to create a name that is nothing more than parts of other words stuck together. For example, the Cleveland area alone boasts such firms as Comtech, Infotech, Newtech, Teletech, Telecom, Comtel, and Computel. Compare these computer-oriented names to the distinctive Gateway Inc., with its black-and-white spots insignia, or Macintosh, with its apple logo. And yes, both Gateway and Macintosh (Apple Corp.) started as home-based businesses, too.

One of my favorite name-change success stories is told by Kaile Warren, Jr., who renamed his home-repair business Rent-a-Husband Inc. Although he quips that "a lot of people thought I had an escort service," the name change combined with targeting a specific audience (women aged twenty-five to fifty) transformed his Portland, Maine, business into a million-dollar nationwide franchise operation. And the name change landed him spots on the Montel Williams and Maury Povich shows.

◆ **Drop general references.** Avoid overly general monikers like American, General, United, National, Federal, and U.S. The words are too commonplace and add no distinction or value to your name. Could this be why Continental Oil Company became Conoco, American Information Technologies Corp. became Ameritech, and American National Corporation became Amcorp? In metro Seattle alone, there are more than 110 General, 300 National, and 450 American entries in the yellow pages (I chose to research general references in

Seattle due to its distance from Washington, D.C., where such references thrive). I once had an executive from America West in one of my training classes who said her company is always being confused with American Airlines and the shuttle service American Eagle.

Additionally, commonplace words such as American and National do not provide much legal protection. After your public shortens your name, as they will if it's too long, you may end up being known by a name that you cannot claim. Western Hotels, a worldwide hotel chain, learned that they could not prevent competitors from using "Western" in their names, so they changed Western to Westin.

In some situations, however, depending upon your services, I could be persuaded that these add-ons might help your company appear larger. There is, after all, a marketing concept known as *preconceived market perception,* in which consumers assume they have heard of a company even if it is new. Generally, the familiarity derives from use of common words such as American, Eastern, General, and so on. For example, if you lived in Georgia and wanted to sell business equipment across your state *and* never wanted to expand beyond that territory *and* the name was legally available, then you could call your company Georgia Business Machines, taking advantage of consumers' familiarity with International Business Machines (IBM). The thinking is that Georgia Business Machines would be assumed by the general public to be a subsidiary of IBM. But as with IBM, whose name was shortened by the masses, you might find your public abbreviating your name. . . if it registered with them at all, since it is needlessly long. So scrap general references.

◆ **D.U.A.A.P. (Don't use abbreviations or acronyms, please.)** Yes, I recognize that they have been especially popular in the past several years—all the more reason to avoid them. Acronyms are becoming a naming fad, and in a few years, we're going to see those acronymed companies undertaking expensive name changes. Besides, you would have to spend a lot of money to tell your customers what the acronym stands for. And finally, even reasonably intelligent people often have a hard time finding abbreviations in alphabetical lists of names, such as those in buyer's directories and yellow pages.

Besides, the only acronyms that truly work are those that have a meaning relevant to the product or purpose they promote; for example, MADD (Mothers Against Drunk Driving) is a very powerful and appropriate acronym.

◆ **Think big. Think internationally.** It used to be that when someone started a new business, people would laugh at the entrepreneur's affirmation that she would be doing business internationally. Now, with the ease of doing business around the world, an entrepreneur should be laughed at for *not* thinking globally right from the start.

Had Chevrolet checked names for international appeal and acceptance prior to launching the Nova in Mexico, the company would have learned that Nova sounds like a Spanish phrase for "doesn't go." Would you buy a car that carries that distinction? Thus, think of global interpretations and meanings when you name your company and products.

◆ **Consider a coined word.** The advantage? It offers better legal protection and unrestricted growth opportunities. The disadvantage? You may have to spend a lot of money to build recognition because customers will be uncomfortable with a name that to them has no meaning.

Navistar, Primerica, Xerox, Exxon, and UNISYS are familiar coined names. Primerica, for example, was a good choice for the company that adopted it because the old name had nothing to do with the company's present focus: financial services. Reeducating the public would have cost much more than taking on a new name. The old name of the company? American Can.

SPECIAL CONSIDERATIONS

◆ **Play with all possible abbreviations, definitions, and pronunciations.** Look for novel ways to keep your name short, fun, and memorable. Weed out names with double or negative meanings. I've actually seen companies with these names: Feyasco Convention Planning and Vorhaus (pronounced Vor-house) Property Management.

◆ **Know when to use your own name.** Should you use your own name? It depends. If you're well known in your field already and are going to open a consulting firm, you may want to bank on the reputation you've already established. If, however, you're opening a new business to sell products or provide a service in which you haven't yet established an expertise, then, in general, using your name is not a good idea.

My friend Denise Dudley is the copresident and cofounder of SkillPath Seminars. She and her husband, Jerry Brown, have turned the company into a $130 million business over the past ten years. Both had begun establishing themselves as seminar leaders and trainers in parts of the United States before launching their business. However, being determined and farsighted entrepreneurs, they knew that they wanted "to offer training internationally," Denise says. "So we knew we needed a name that would suggest the achievement we wanted our clients to feel after attending one of our seminars. And we wanted to name it *once,* so we wanted a name with longevity."

Sure, it's true that surnames worked wonders for other giants: Ford, Rockefeller, Kennedy, Armani, Gillette. But those names have built equity over the years and have become inseparable from the products they produce. In general, if you're going to use your name, then the shorter your last name, the better. Don't use hyphenated or long names or ones that are difficult to spell or pronounce.

Too many architectural and engineering firms (and attorneys) use their last names, resulting in long names that carry too many syllables and commas. While I was in Denver conducting a training seminar, I turned to the U.S. West Metro Denver yellow pages and randomly placed my finger on the architect listings. My finger touched two firms: Affinity Design Group and Agnes, Anderson and Scholl Architecture. Now, if you're moving from out of town and don't have much time to research credentials, who are you going to call first? I don't know a thing about Agnes, Anderson, or Scholl, but I do like the feeling I get from the idea of having affinity with my new home. Conclusion? Affinity Design Group must strive to achieve harmony between home and home owner. They'd get my business.

◆ **Avoid "& Associates" and articles.** If you do use your own name, there's often the temptation to make it "John Smith & Associates" to suggest size. This might make sense in some cases, but in general "& Associates" is overused. Most prospective clients today know that the company can be as small as a solo John Smith, and they will interpret the "& Associates" as "& No Employees."

Also think twice before using articles such as *The* and *A*. Customers will automatically add them when referring to your company, yet they won't think to consider them when looking for you in the yellow pages, and it's hard to tell where your listing might end up.

◆ **Register your name.** Make your name legal—nationally, at a minimum. Do it before you spend any money on advertising, stationery, or signs. Imagine launching your business and, in the last-minute rush of registration, finding out that the name has to be discarded because a legal search turned up a prior registration or a potential infringement. Remember, though, that registering your business name is a local or state process and is completely separate from registering a trademark nationally.

Although you are not required legally to register your name in other states or localities, you will find it good business to register your name as a trademark either nationally or in several states to prevent other businesses from using the name. Even if you plan to stay in your geographic area, that does not preclude another company with the same trade name or trademark from moving into your area. That company might be able to force you to stop doing business under the name.

◆ **Incorporate yourself, if appropriate.** An "Inc." distinction makes your company look bigger and more official. Other advantages of incorporating include a potentially lower tax rate, protection for personal assets, and ease of attracting investors. Incorporating generally costs less than $300, and you don't need an attorney to do it. You can find the appropriate forms in many office-supply stores. For information specific to your state and local area, check with the Small Business Administration (SBA). Call the SBA information line at 800-827-5722 for the office nearest to you.

Your Company's Address

HAVING A BETTER PRODUCT OR SERVICE THAN YOUR BIGGER competitors won't do you any good if potential customers can't find you (if they come to you) or are skeptical of your address (if you go to them). Where you set up shop and how you describe that location will reflect upon the image you're trying to create.

IF CUSTOMERS COME TO YOU

◆ **Make sure you are easy to find.** List yourself in all the appropriate and logical places. While it's true that word-of-mouth referrals make the best new business, generally all that carries from person to person is your company's name, not your address, phone number, or business card. Will the person in need be able to find you in any of the locations he would logically look? If not, he'll immediately begin to get the impression that you are small. The more he searches, the more unimpressed he will be, until he finally will give up. Don't overlook yellow page listings, industry directories, professional references, the chamber of commerce, and Internet search engines.

◆ **Choose the best location.** Regardless of your line of business, location is important to the image you're trying to create. Generally, the company that can deliver the goods the fastest, least-expensive way will get the contract. If you operate a consulting firm and your clients are spread throughout the country, you can offer significantly lower prices if you live near a major airport, because it won't cost clients as much money to get you to their offices. If you plan to set up a shop to manufacture a product, you will want to consider your accessibility to suppliers and to transportation for reaching customers. Shipping charges can add up quickly. If you're looking for a shop customers will visit, then you should do a careful demographic study of population statistics, labor force availability, per capita income, education level, and other important statistical information, which is available from the library, the chamber of commerce, or census records.

Should you locate near the competition? It depends on your business and the demographics working for and against you. If, for example, you want to open a car dealership, you may find it wise to set up shop beside your competition. Automobile dealers locate together to take advantage of one another's customer traffic. If your town has a dealership mall on the east side of town and you set up on the west side, not only will customers ignore you, since you're not convenient for comparison shopping, but you also will emphasize your size. Ever notice that when several dealerships are together, they all look big because it's hard to tell where one ends and the other begins?

◆ **Look at leasing.** If you're thinking of leasing a facility for a business with customer traffic, do a careful study of that space first. Sure, there may be a busy grocery store two stores down from where you want to set up shop, but if that's the store drawing the crowds, you may be out of luck. Buyers won't put their groceries in their cars and then shop leisurely for items like computers, vacation packages, and wallpaper. Besides, who feels like spending more money after they've seen their grocery bill? You should decide whether a grocery store is in line with the buying disposition you want in your customers. For card shops and drug stores, it usually is.

◆ **Make parking available.** One of the biggest problems for small businesses with a storefront is trying to compete with the accessibility that bigger businesses provide. If you're searching for a shop now, don't consider any location that will require customers to park across the street. If you already have a shop and parking is not convenient, get creative! Offer validated parking privileges at nearby lots, hand out maps showing prime parking spots, or offer a prize each day to the customer who has the worst parking story to tell.

◆ **Keep your shop orderly and clean.** Ever notice how as a business grows and image becomes established, some companies become too comfortable, perhaps even careless? First you notice extra boxes or stacks of files lying around, then you notice the plants are ignored and dying, and finally you begin to experience the disorganization as you wait for employees to find things. Makes you wonder who's in charge and why he doesn't notice the mess. If you can't be objective about your shop and its physical presentation anymore, then ask an acquaintance to stop in and give you an honest opinion. And *always* make sure there are no missing letters or bulbs in your sign. That is the most visible tip-off that your business lacks proper attention.

IF YOU WORK FROM HOME

MAKE SURE YOU COMPLY WITH ALL ZONING LAWS. DESPITE THE existence of millions of home-based businesses, entrepreneurs still suffer from outdated, conflicting, discriminatory, and poorly written zoning ordinances. Unfortunately, nothing could be more harmful to your image than to be mentioned in the local paper as fighting a zoning law that keeps you from operating a business in your home. You may be presented as a hero who is politically involved, but the news coverage will alert your customers about how small you are. You have to decide whether in your line of work that revelation will hurt or help you.

Of course, you can do what countless other entrepreneurs have told me they've done: ignore the laws. I'll share my favorite story here that one business owner told me, but I'll give him a fake surname and company name. Jeff Perrin, founder of Sports and Playworld, told me he started working at home because he wanted to *be* at home. So when his company grew so large that he was forced to move his business from his home due to zoning, he rented a storage building to establish a commercial address. "I received deliveries there and actually kept most of my inventory there," Jeff says. "At night, however, I'd load up my car and drive back to my house, where the paper-flow portion of my business remained. When I filled my next batch of orders, I went back to the storage building for more."

Another entrepreneur I know who founded a direct-marketing company in New York worked at his kitchen table; however, through a business support group he rented a Madison Avenue address for $200 a month to appear larger to his clients and to avoid zoning problems.

◆ **Study your home-business address carefully.** If you have a business-friendly street address (it sounds professional as opposed to tranquil and serene), use it instead of a post office box. A housing development near me hosts streets called Abiding Way Drive and Magnolia Blossom Lane. Home owners on these roads who wish to set up home offices should opt for a mailbox at the post office or through a mail-service store. Also, if you use mailing stores and services, such as Mail Boxes, Etc., you can rent their street address.

◆ **If it's most practical, then get a post office box.**
Reasons *for* a post office box:
—Separates your business mail from your personal mail.
—Sometimes post office boxes receive mail faster than street addresses.
—For security reasons: you can shield your home address from your business contacts.
—Some large companies do use post office boxes.
—Your street address may shout "suburban neighborhood."
Reasons *against* a post office box:
—They have a reputation as being used by small businesses.
—You will have to go there to retrieve mail every day.
—Overnight package delivery services will not deliver to a box number.

◆ **If you retain your home address, consider adding a suite number.** Not only does it sound more professional, but it also will help to separate personal from business mail. If you live in an apartment building, use *Suite 200* rather than *Apt. 200*. The post office will still deliver your mail, and it will appear that you are in an office building or office park.

KNOW YOUR STRENGTHS
AND WEAKNESSES

UNDERSTANDING YOURSELF CAN
HELP YOU BE MORE COMPETITIVE

NOW THAT YOU'VE NAMED AND LOCATED YOUR BUSINESS, what's next? Before you make any changes, spend any money, or identify new directions, you need to look at your personal strengths and weaknesses and determine how to work with—or around—them to accomplish the goals you set for your business.

Surprisingly, one of the biggest challenges you may have to overcome in order to compete is your very nature as an entrepreneur. The same entrepreneurial traits that are going to motivate you and your passion—your business—are also going to be at the root of your most frustrating moments. Recognizing when you are playing entrepreneur rather than one of the many other roles you must perform—for example, salesperson, human resources director, marketing specialist—will help you make the temporary transition into those roles when necessary.

Look at your competitors. They are not made up exclusively of leaders. Their accounting departments are filled with employees whose passion is numbers. Their marketing staffs are expert with words or people. They have engineers who prefer to work with things. Big companies are made up of people whose personalities match the tasks that must be accomplished. Because you're a small business, you probably don't yet have that privilege. You are not—and can't be—expert in all these fields.

Many entrepreneurs are especially bad at operating certain parts of their business. They should probably work *on* their business more than they work *in* their business. If this describes you, then you're going to need the right people to help you as soon as possible. Until you can afford to hire, however, you will have to adapt to the many roles you must assume. It helps if you know how you differ from the people who perform the many equivalent tasks for the big companies.

The following description of an entrepreneur comes not only from my experience—my familiarity with entrepreneurs' strengths and foibles comes from being one myself—but also from having coached and consulted for other entrepreneurs. That's when I learned the most about how the same personality that can drive you can also cause you to stumble.

How Entrepreneurs Differ from Other People

WE'VE ALL HEARD OF THE "CREATIVE" TYPE, AND WE'VE LEARNed that creative people do things in their own ways and that others have to make exceptions (or excuses) for their differences. Well, like it or not, entrepreneurs are very creative people who generate ideas continually and develop them through one or more businesses.

Entrepreneurs don't understand how anyone could be happy being a dental hygienist, for example: operating in the same small space for years, cleaning teeth, never having any prospects for anything bigger than the going rate for hygienists. Entrepreneurs overlook the job stability and security, the benefits, the comfortable working conditions, and the reward of helping others. Sure, entrepreneurs want all that, but not if the price they must pay to get it is monotonous work *for someone else*. Likewise, entrepreneurs don't understand the total devotion of health professionals and teachers, either. Their satisfaction comes from building a company from nothing—developing a product or service and watching it grow to unlimited heights.

An awareness of this outlook on work and life should help you throttle back on your opinions when you're with a client. Even if your prospect is not a dental hygienist or a teacher or a member of any one of hundreds of professions that differ from yours, your prospect's spouse or child or parent might be. It's a good idea to keep your opinions and your value system in check.

Here are some more differences between entrepreneurs

(Es) and other people: Es start new projects continuously; other people take reasonable breaks between projects. Es need to make a lot of money to feel successful; other people just enjoy making money and feel successful because they make that money. Es often look at people as things to use to get what they want; other people see people as friends and acquaintances to enjoy (only a select group of people in the latter category make the "fit" as entrepreneurs). Es tend to be loners, because they enjoy time to think and because other people are too slow and don't "understand" them. Es are resourceful at getting whatever it is they need, even the trust of other people. Es can seem very insecure and have a hard time taking criticism.

Many of these traits describe me, too, but it wasn't until I began coaching and consulting with entrepreneurs that I realized just how different we were. I've found that entrepreneurs learn and grow as they speak, not as they listen. That could be one reason my former partner always chided me for repeating conversations; I had to talk to find my answer, my comfort, my solution, my end result. Speaking over listening is a bad trait in sales, however. So although talking a lot may help you *plot* your business, it's not going to help you sell your business. The advantage, then, that bigger companies have over you is that they have people who sell *and* people who manage and direct, and generally the right personalities are in the right places.

Entrepreneurs are never satisfied. They constantly feel that they haven't accomplished enough, because they constantly get new ideas. As long as they have an idea that they haven't acted upon or built into a company, they feel that they have failed. Surprisingly, most entrepreneurs would be happiest if they could start a dozen companies and turn each one over as soon as it had grown to the point at which someone else could run it for them. One of the best things I do for my clients is to help them realize that they're going to get hundreds of ideas for businesses in their lifetimes and that they need to let go of most of them.

How does this penchant for constant idea generation affect your image? One way is that your enthusiasm generally surfaces at the wrong times, such as when you're with a client. I've seen many entrepreneurs, self-made consultants, and wanna-bes who have won jobs with big companies and then unconsciously revealed their restlessness with their current project through their reaction to ideas they get. I once had an assignment to audit a large-scale crisis plan for a Midwest nuclear facility. Because I was not an expert in one of the many aspects of the audit, radiation plume tracking, I hired a man who was. He had his own firm and a tremendous reputation. But while at the facility, he noticed that certain stockpiles of piping were going to be wasted because they didn't meet the stringent standards set by the federal government for nuclear facilities. He knew other industries would be more than happy to get the pipes at a discount price. What do you suppose he plotted and discussed most while at this assignment? Not plume tracking. He had another agenda and yet another business developing in his head. My client was unimpressed, so I quickly let him go.

Entrepreneurs also have a hard time with structure, preferring to devote attention to the parts of a business that interest them the most. I've discovered that structure is one of the best things I give my entrepreneurial clients: the regular check-in, the phone call, the development (and reminder) of life goals, the framework of organization, and the accountability when needed. This structure contributes to momentum. Without structure and momentum, entrepreneurs—like other creative types—wouldn't know which course to follow.

The life plan must come before the business plan. My friend Julia Starr learned this the hard way: "My partner and I wanted a highly successful company, and that was it. If anyone asked me what I wanted out of life, the only answer I had was about my company. Why I wanted it, I didn't know; I was simply determined to have it. And I got it. But my family life became stressful. I was constantly torn between work and my child. I barely spoke with cherished relatives and friends. My partner and I lost sight of the joy of the business. We let it come between our companionship, and because of certain ways he reacted to the situation, the trust broke

Quick Review of the
Entrepreneur's (E's) Personality

GENERAL OBSERVATIONS

1 Es love to make money, as opposed to people who make money to do things they love.
2 Es have bigger dreams than other people.
3 Es are very success oriented.
4 Es are restless, and therefore their impatience with people, situations, and meetings often shows.
5 Es work harder than most people because, at times, they're not sure whether it's work or play.
6 Es are better at something than most people.
7 Es look at risks differently than most folks.
8 Es are very proud and therefore can be more easily annoyed or insulted than others.
9 Es have a smaller but tighter circle of friends than most people.
10 Es have a lower tolerance for office politics, gossip, and water-cooler discussions.

COMMON TRAITS

1 One or both parents was self-employed.
2 Many Es have been fired one or more times.
3 Es generally go into business at a young age.
4 Most Es are less than 45 years old.
5 Es are usually the oldest child in the family; the status of youngest child comes in second.
6 The majority are married.
7 Most have at least a bachelor's degree.
8 Es are very sociable people when necessary; otherwise, they tend to be loners.
9 Es are superorganized but often need help with structure.
10 Es are highly competitive.

down, and we lost a valued relationship. When I took time off to write a book, my partner, unbeknownst to me until too late, begrudged my time away from the business. And finally, I experienced a health problem; although it was easily corrected in the end, apparently I had been experiencing it for quite a while without even realizing it due to my stress and unhappiness. Had I developed a life plan and been faithful to it *before* or even *when* my company became successful, the personal aspects of my life might not have suffered. When those began to suffer, my professional life, of course, began to suffer. Clients can always pick up on that."

Is Your Attitude Talking?

A CLIENT I COACHED ONCE TOLD ME THAT HE HAD JUST HAD A terrible fight with his supplier, and because his order was small, he feared it would be put off until the last minute. The supplier accused my client of having an attitude problem. To this, my angry and very proud client yelled, "I don't have an attitude problem; you have a perception problem."

Although it was a clever comeback, I knew that he had just alienated himself from someone necessary to his business. As a small business owner, you cannot afford to do this. Your business is growing, so you must develop a positive attitude and apply it to every aspect of your work. You must be in control of yourself and each situation. It's not what happens to you but rather how you handle it that distinguishes you professionally.

A positive attitude sees opportunity everywhere; a negative attitude sees only hardship and overlooks opportunity. My client saw only adversity and lashed out in reaction. What he should have seen was a problem that, if handled with diplomacy, could have impressed his supplier enough that he would have put my client at the top of his list for the perks and favors his other clients don't enjoy. I've seen it happen.

Small businesses rarely succeed when their founders are pessimists, overly skeptical, or too narrowly focused. You have to believe in yourself, your product, and your mission.

When you see an opportunity, you must leap at it. Unlike most entrepreneurs, I began my former business with a cautious attitude. It took me a couple of years to develop and enjoy the I-can-do-anything positive attitude that my former partner had. He was the eternal optimist when it came to building our firm. Many was the time we would sit in meetings with potential clients and agree to take on work we'd never done before. This was also my introduction to ethics versus belief in yourself. Upon leaving the meeting, I would invariably ask, "How are we going to do that?" and his response was always, "Beats the heck out of me, but we will." And we always did. And we did it well. I soon came to learn that he believed in himself, in me, in us to be able to do the job, whereas I originally thought he might have been pushing the ethical line a bit too much. Of course, when the assignment was too unrelated to our expertise, we did say no, which helped us build credibility.

Always remember how you want to be perceived, and conduct yourself accordingly. You should be proud of what you do, so display an air of confidence and satisfaction. Successful people are content, secure, happy, proud, and undaunted. You want your clients immediately to recognize your confidence and competence. Let your presentation, appearance, and demeanor tell your audience that you are the best, and make sure that everything you do and say reflects your image as a winner. With persistence, the description you claim will become accepted truth.

Honesty Is the Best Business Policy

I'LL NEVER FORGET HOW I GOT MY FIRST CLIENT AS A BUSIness coach. I met Charles years ago on a flight from Boston to Cleveland. Charles was one of four partners in a telecommunications firm. After sharing stories about our work and our start-up days, I revealed that I wanted to build a separate coaching practice someday to help clients optimize their personal and professional lives. I told him how I planned to train for the role and simultaneously begin writing about my business experience. He shared with me what was on his mind those days: one of his partners, Ned, had asked him to lie to a client. According to Charles, he felt compelled to do as Ned asked, because Ned was a very disagreeable person who never trusted anything his three partners were doing. Charles hoped that by making the man happy, he could begin to establish more of an agreeable atmosphere with him. Charles asked me what I thought he should do.

Although I thought his intentions and his heart were in the right place, I thought his integrity and reputation might be jeopardized, so I said, "I wouldn't do it. I would tell this guy, 'I'm not going to lie *for* you, because then you'll think that I could lie *to* you.'" About four weeks later, I received a letter from Charles that read, "Thank you for coaching me on a potentially damaging situation. I followed your advice, and the partner has actually gained respect for me. When we partners had our last meeting, Ned kept asking me what I thought and voting however I voted. When you start your coaching business, let me know."

Most of us were brought up to tell the truth, but then we enter the business world, and we learn to politely finesse and negotiate the facts. Some entrepreneurs learn the art of white lies, half-truths, and honesty on a need-to-please basis. I see it happen a lot. When entrepreneurs are on their own, they enjoy the freedom to set their own ethical agendas, because there's no powerhouse company keeping tabs on their honesty. It takes a strong, self-assured, and confident entrepreneur to stick with the truth, because it's so easy to lie. The problem is that if you lie, you might be caught, and then all credibility is gone. There's a good reason that these two sayings have stood the test of time: "Dishonesty introduces a man to himself," and "The liar's punishment is not that he is not believed but that he can believe no one else."

But keep in mind that telling the truth *at the wrong time and unnecessarily* can be just as damaging as lying. Entrepreneurs who open up too much to show how aboveboard they are end up confusing frankness with honesty and gush too much sincerity: "Things have been really slow lately, so I really appreciate your business." This candor may seem refreshing to you, but it will reveal you to be hungry and desperate for work, which is not a good negotiating position to be in.

Not only are lies unethical, but they are too hard to remember! I confess that in my early days I told a white lie. I thought we had to "enhance" our staff size to be competitive. I rationalized by saying that I was only massaging the truth, not lying. At the time, we were a full-time staff of two, part-time of three, and had dozens of associates that we used periodically. Couldn't we, therefore, justifiably say we had dozens working for us? Soon it became hard to remember which company thought we had dozens of employees, which thought we had two, and which knew the full truth. I found it easier and obviously more ethical just to tell the truth all the time.

Honesty always comes back to bless me with a competitive advantage, too. For example, years ago I found $250 in cash along with a car rental discount coupon in an envelope in an airport gate waiting area. Of course I thought of all the wonderful restaurants where I could eat on this business trip thanks to my newfound loot, but I was plagued with thoughts that the money might belong to an out-of-work single mom traveling to visit her dying child in a distant hospital. Eight phone calls (only three of which were toll-free) to airlines and car rental agencies later, I was no closer to finding the owner. On the ninth call, I happened to link up with the owner of a car rental franchise who was so impressed with my honesty that he kept talking, and we exchanged backgrounds. Years later I landed consulting work with him. Had I been an employee of a large company, he would have known that he could trust me but not necessarily the company. Because I was owner of a small firm, he immediately trusted my entire company, since I was in charge.

How Do You Describe Yourself?

TRY THIS EXERCISE TO DETERMINE HOW EFFECTIVE YOUR RUDImentary marketing skills are: Ask a dozen friends and acquaintances—your neighbors or parents in your child's school or people you know through sports teams or social clubs—to briefly describe your business.

Are you surprised by their answers? How accurate were their descriptions? Could they describe you well to others they meet? Or did you find yourself providing more information or a simpler explanation?

The problem could be twofold: (1) You haven't practiced the "three-foot rule." Because your number-one marketing tool is yourself, you should be telling everyone within three feet of you about your company and its services or products. You'll read more about how to deal with friends and family in Chapter 2; and (2) You haven't articulated what you do in a clear, easily understandable, and memorable way. It's this latter problem we'll tackle here.

Creating a descriptive statement about your company is smart business. Most people understand what big companies (your competitors) do because their expensive advertisements educate the public. But you don't have that privilege, so the education will have to come directly from you. Your descriptive statement should answer as many of the following questions as possible:

◆ Who are you?
◆ What business are you in?
◆ How do you want to be perceived?
◆ What clientele do you serve?
◆ With whom are you competing?
◆ What makes you different from your competitors?
◆ What benefits does a customer derive from your services?

The catch is that you should be able to deliver this statement within fifteen to thirty seconds, the same amount of time that you might spend riding an elevator from one floor to another. Why? Because that's about how long you have in any introductory situation to clearly explain yourself and your company. If you've prepared a powerful statement, someone might ask to hear more. The ideal introduction captivates the listener's interest, gives a positive impression, and creates a link between you and your product or service.

Creating a brief and powerful introduction begins with identifying situations or problems your prospects have that you can solve. For example, one of the many hats I wear is that of copresident of WriteDirections.com. My introduction might go something like this: "I am copresident of Write-Directions.com, which I'm proud to say is the only virtual writing institute of its kind. We provide coaching and consulting, and almost forty telephone and Internet classes to move writers in the direction they want and need to go. If you work with us, whether you're a writer or a specialist in any field who needs to write, you will work with professional writers to accomplish your writing goals, including everything from writing a winning news release or marketing brochure to preparing an effective book proposal or novel." Thus, I make it clear that our company helps to solve any problems people may have with writing.

Another hat I wear is that of business and writing coach. My coaching skills are versatile and easily applicable to anyone with almost any type of need, so do the areas I specialize in matter as much during an introduction as what a coach does? No, because with the division between personal and business life blurring, the coach is the only professional trained to work with all the many roles a person plays. But if I simply say that I'm a coach, my acquaintances might not understand what that is. You might find, as I have, that you need to develop several introductory statements to best speak to the person you're addressing: "You're familiar with what a coach does for an athlete? Then you know it's the athlete who has the ability to make the goal or win the medal, but without the coach to provide structure and direction and to encourage and guide the athlete, he would have a much harder time achieving his best. I do something similar for people in their daily lives. Wouldn't you love to have a coach beside you helping you to concentrate on your goals and to become the best that you can be? That's what I do for people." This brevity and clarity allows my friends to find potential clients for me, because they have a clear way of communicating what I do. This is important, because to sell effectively and efficiently, nothing works as well as getting others to spread endorsements on your behalf.

When you hear that great American line "What do you do?" one technique is to ask whether the other person is familiar with the key annoyances or problems addressed by your business, then explain that your business eliminates or solves them. If you're a builder of custom homes, for example, your introduction might sound something like this: "I'm a custom builder. Do you know when you drive into a development how all the homes look alike? Well, you'll never see my name associated with those, because I design and build homes that are uniquely tailored to my clients' personalities and needs." Upon hearing this, even if you don't have the budget now for a custom-designed home, wouldn't you ask for this guy's card for future reference? This is much more impressive than if he had just said, "I'm a custom builder."

If this same custom builder had the time and obvious attention of listeners, he could go on to say, "Custom homes are within anyone's budget. It doesn't necessarily mean expensive, it just means custom. For example, I had a client recently who. . . ." Then he could mention a job that would be similar to what the listeners might consider for themselves.

By discussing what he did for a client, the custom builder established a hook that will stay in prospects' minds long after he's met them. Adding the example of one client's experiences provides a story that is much more meaningful than facts and figures that people could pick up anywhere.

Here's another example of describing your services in terms of the problems you solve: A friend of mine near Cleveland recently started a shuttle service for children. When she's introduced, however, she doesn't rattle off the fact that she charges X dollars per mile to haul a child from one place to another. Instead she says, "I help ease the burden of busy parents who, because of work or other obligations, can't pick up their child from day care or music lessons or sporting events. I shuttle those children from one place to another under contract so that the parent never has to worry about the child's safety." Wouldn't you agree that there's a big difference between offering to help a concerned parent juggle work and family life and saying you haul kids for a fee?

I've heard some pithy and whimsical introductions through the years. A caterer once told me that he would make me "a guest at your own party." He got the job. A cleaning service once hooked me when they explained, "We don't cut corners, we scrub them." Then there's the exterminator who says he'll take care of "anything that's bugging you," and the mortgage company that claims "It's in our interest to save you interest." When you meet clever people like this—assuming their price and credentials are in line— you want to reward their creativity with a job, don't you?

Keep Educating Your Current Clients

THERE'S AN OLD ADAGE THAT 80 PERCENT OF YOUR REVENUE will come from 20 percent of your clients. Knowing this, doesn't it make sense to keep reminding existing clients what services or products you offer?

Jay Massey, president of Coco Design Associates in Pensacola, Florida, will never again forget that message: "We had one client who, after we delivered an eight-page, full-color brochure to them, went to another firm for help with trade show display graphics and a revision to their logo. It was my fault, because I failed to communicate to them that we were a full-service agency. Fortunately, they were floored when they learned the price charged by the other company. Now they turn to us when they need any design help; however, I learned to make sure all our clients know what services we offer."

Jay says that he failed to communicate that his company was a full-service agency; yet I can attest that even if you use that phrase, customers may not know what it means. I used to tell clients that my company was a full-service crisis management firm. I knew exactly what that meant and assumed anyone shopping for crisis management expertise would, too. Imagine my dismay when, as we were preparing a plan for one large company in Columbus, Ohio, our contact came to me and said we were welcome to sit in on the upcoming crisis communication training. Our client had contracted another company to train their communication staff on how to work with the news media during an emergency. After my client learned that crisis communication was my specialty and that he could have factored the cost of the training into the contract, he got frustrated with us. Lesson learned: Continually, but diplomatically, spell out for your clients the full extent of your services or product line.

All Work and No Play Makes a Grumpy Entrepreneur

WHY WOULD I WRITE ABOUT TAKING THE TIME TO PLAY AND relax in a book about working hard enough to outsmart your competition? The simple answer is that if you don't find a good balance in your life, you won't be as effective with your clients, and you won't be as interesting to them, either. It's important to your personal health and to the health of your business to maintain a stable balance and a stable attitude. Nonstop work actually harms the creativity and productivity that are essential to success.

You've got a situation to tackle that the employees at your bigger competitors don't have: you have to work longer, harder, and smarter than they do because you're covering *all* the bases of your company. If you are a home-based business owner, you have to relax in the same location, too. Since the Internet and international business require you to be open twenty-four hours a day, your efforts to relax may seem futile. And judging by the time that was stamped on many phone and e-mail messages I received from friends and contacts regarding interviews for this book, I would say that many entrepreneurs are overworked.

You should practice the following principles:

◆ **Develop self-discipline about *not* working.** "I learned a long time ago that I had to walk away from my work and take care of myself mentally and physically and then come back to it," one financial consultant told me. "If I didn't, I would lose my edge with clients." She also noted that the initial attempt to work at home was very draining on her. "I had to continually reassess what I should be doing. I would fight with myself all morning not to do household tasks like cleaning and yard work, but then when six o'clock rolled around, I had to fight with myself to go do that cleaning and yard work instead of returning just one more client call."

◆ **Set and keep business hours.** Not only will you avoid burnout, but you'll eliminate the impression that you are a hobbyist rather than a business owner. Regular hours tell your clients that you are serious about business.

◆ **Establish boundaries.** One client I consulted with came to me for my marketing expertise, yet I quickly surmised that he was in threat of burnout because of all that he was trying to accomplish in one day. I knew that he needed to get his schedule in order before he could effectively deal with marketing. He had left his corporate job so that he could work at home, develop a business in a field that motivated him, see his kids more, and have more control over his life. Yet because he wasn't setting boundaries on his schedule, he wasn't accomplishing any of his goals. In fact, his attempt to do it all stressed him so much that his kids soon didn't want him around, he began to resent the hours he was keeping, and he realized he had no control over his life. The dilemma was especially perplexing to him because he was a tax consultant and therefore felt he should be able to keep "regular" business hours. Together, we devised a new schedule that works for him and his family. He wakes up early, because his clients know they can call him as early as 6 A.M. By 8 A.M., he's eating breakfast with his two boys before they leave for school at 9. At 1 P.M., he's feeling overwhelmed from four hours of solid work, so he takes a midday break to jog five miles, which helps to rejuvenate him physically *and* mentally. After that, he eats lunch and puts in two hours of work before his boys get home from school. Then he takes an hour off to play with them. Afterward, he does filing and other administrative work that is easily interruptible until dinner. After dinner with his family, he makes calls to a client on the West Coast and one in Alaska.

◆ **Change your perspective.** The tax consultant had to alter his thinking before he could appreciate his new situation and move on to operating his business effectively. After we finished developing his schedule and *before* he tried it out, he begrudged the fact that he would be working from 6 A.M. until 9 P.M. each day. Then he tried it and realized that when he was at his corporate job, he was up at 6 A.M. anyway to prepare for a long commute to work. He had also had no interaction with his family until 6 P.M. when he was too tired to enjoy it, and after the kids went to bed, he never felt like exercising. His new schedule gave him what he wanted in divided blocks of time, and it best accommodated a clientele in several time zones.

◆ **Find a balance.** One of the things I love to do most is writing. But I also enjoy public speaking and sharing my knowledge with others. So if I'm asked to give a presentation or conduct a class, the amount of money involved needs to justify the amount of time I will need to invest. This keeps me focused on writing, consulting, and being with my son, Matthew. When the job involves travel, I make sure the pay justifies my time away from him and from the work I love. But when I do travel, I make the most of it. I make every trip a minivacation, because I'm a firm believer that life is made up of appreciated moments. If it hadn't been for this philosophy and a few minutes of preplanning before each business trip, I would have missed out on moments like these, just in the United States and Canada alone: a breathtaking meteor shower in northeast Wisconsin, whale watching off the coast of Maine, ice-skating at an Olympic training center in Milwaukee, center-front seats for *The Phantom of the Opera* in Toronto, countless shows on Broadway, art exhibits in Philadelphia, incredible planetarium shows in Chicago and Atlanta, the best seafood I've ever had in Boston, Chinese food just about everywhere I go, and one of the most memorable moments of my life—walking along a pier in Santa Monica on a warm evening and rounding a corner to see three teenage boys playing Pachelbel's Canon in D on their string instruments. The moment was so magical it brought tears to my eyes. Instead of resenting my absence from my son at those times, I enjoyed them, knowing that upon my return such moments would make me a better mom to him, because it's impossible to teach him to achieve balance in his life if I don't do it myself. And these experiences gave me colorful stories and anecdotes to share with clients over lunch.

◆ **Schedule similar tasks together.** One of my friends thinks she has hit upon the solution to running her desktop publishing business: she has workdays and errand days. On workdays, she never leaves the office. On errand days, she schedules back-to-back appointments and meetings. "When I have errands to do and jobs to deliver, my schedule is thrown off, and so is my concentration," she says. "I've solved that by doing all my errands on the same day, leaving me free to work uninterrupted on other days."

◆ **Set priorities.** And finally, know and take care of the most important people in your life. At the top of my list is my son, Matthew, and it was the same for my former partner. He was completely devoted to his son, Adam. He told everyone that and proved it through his actions time and time again, being sure always to be home on weekends when Adam was there—no matter what well-paying assignment came along—so that he could enjoy Adam and Adam could have access to his dad. And it's the same for my current partner, Beth. Her family comes first, then her work.

Get a Coach

CONSIDER HIRING A PERSONAL COACH. I'VE TALKED SEVERAL times about coaching in this book, but what does that mean? Before I explain, let me say that this is not an advertisement, because you don't have to hire me. Look up www.CoachU. com or www.TherapyWorld.com on the Internet, and you will find lists of coaches who may fit your personality and your specific needs.

People turn to coaches to help them become more focused and productive. No serious athlete, actor, or performer would expect to progress very far without a coach. A coach can benefit your life by helping you balance your personal life with the development of your company. A coach can lend you the objectivity you need to size up your competition and to set goals for competing with them.

Through working with a coach, you will get your life in such great shape—and become so balanced, happy, and pleased—that your stability becomes obvious to your clients and your prospects, who then will be drawn to you more.

Another reason to work with a coach is that entrepreneurs, in general, don't want to deal with practical stuff like accounting and personnel issues. The best thing you can pay for is an objective coach outside of your business who will guide you and hold you accountable for tackling these tasks and for sticking with goals that you set together.

POLISH YOUR ACT BEFORE TAKING IT ON THE ROAD

BUILDING YOUR IMAGE THROUGH FACE-TO-FACE COMMUNICATION

EVEN IN THIS HIGH-TECH ERA, FACE-TO-FACE MEETINGS ARE still the most popular form of business communication. This means you're going to have to put in an appearance with a client sooner or later. Try to make it sooner, because there's no better way to establish rapport and build trust than by shaking someone's hand and conversing in person.

The problem for many small business owners is that it's easy to get so entrenched in the entrepreneur's lifestyle—with its casual dress, quirky hours, and freedom from regular office rules and routines—that it's easy to forget how polished you must look when you visit a corporate office. Individuality and being your own person are great when you're on your own time but often get in the way of doing business in the typical corporate culture. "Birds of a feather flock together" is an assumption you'd better pay attention to when it comes to your business. Fitting in with your client's culture—in appearance, conversation, attitude, and overall business orientation—will work to your advantage.

Where Should You Meet with Clients?

ALTHOUGH MANY OF MY HOME BUSINESS FRIENDS WOULD disagree with me, I think that you should rarely, if ever, have a client come to your home. From that moment on, your client will picture your home when he sees you or thinks of you. Why would you needlessly remind your client how small you are?

"Frankly, I never invite a client to my home office," says Alan Caruba of the Caruba Organization, a Maplewood, New Jersey, public relations counseling firm. "I deal in services, so I prefer to keep everything on the client's turf. My office is equipped to reach out anywhere to achieve its objectives, so there's no need to bring clients here."

I agree with Caruba that the client's "turf" is the best place to meet. *You* are doing work for *them*, so it's best if you see their environment anyway, especially the first time you meet. If you do more work, then you may want to meet elsewhere, because offices are prone to interruptions.

What do you do if a prospect whom you've not yet met suggests meeting at your place to "get out of the office"? Suggest a backup location, such as a restaurant or coffee shop. It's OK to dine with your clients; in fact, it's a great idea if you can carry it off with aplomb. Sometimes it's easier to establish a relationship with a client in a warm, relaxed environment than in a cold and sterile office. Starbucks or an equivalent local coffee shop is good, as is a luncheon bar in a nice hotel.

Instead of meeting for an expensive, inconvenient, time-consuming lunch, consider meeting for breakfast. Breakfast often fits into a client's time better than lunch or dinner. Hotel breakfast rooms or coffee shops are the best places to meet, because they are not too expensive and are much more appropriate than fast-food restaurants; they also are easily accessible and offer ample parking.

Some clients, however, merit a more formal setting, such as a finer restaurant. Just be sure that it's still conducive to discussing work. Don't go to the priciest restaurants thinking that you will impress your client. Instead, you might look like you have no sense of money, which may prompt clients to wonder if you are charging too much for your products or services. And if you're not going to reveal that you're a solo or small-business act, you might also give the impression that you have no loyalty to your company since you so easily spend money at a pricey place.

Another option is to set up an account with a restaurant or country club near you. Get to know the staff and brief them on how you want meals handled.

Be a generous tipper in restaurants: always over 15 percent. For satisfactory service, for example, 20 percent of your total bill indicates that you feel successful enough to be magnanimous. Just don't overdo your tips to the point of looking like a show-off (or emptying your bank account!). And don't call attention to the tip with time-consuming to-the-penny calculations that switch your focus away from your client.

Of course, all this presumes that you've been building a relationship with a prospect who is receptive to a meeting to discuss your services. If you and your prospect are complete strangers, however, then avoid proposing lunch to sell your services. People don't want to be put in a position that makes them think they are going to hear a sales pitch. Instead, give an invitation for a lunch to get opinions or advice.

When Meeting with a Client for the First or Twentieth Time

YOU'VE MARKETED YOURSELF ADROITLY. YOU HANDED YOUR business card to the right person at the right company, and now you have a call to schedule a meeting. Congratulations! You've managed your information flow well in that you've given enough details to intrigue, but not enough for the prospective client to make an informed decision without meeting you.

Now what do you do? Should you say that any time is suitable? Should you walk into the meeting unprepared so that you can present a fresh approach? Should you plan to promise them the sun, moon, and stars if only they'll hire you or buy from you?

Obviously, these tactics are misguided. It's easy to figure out what *not* to do, but not as simple to figure out what to do. Here are some tips:

◆ **Don't be too available.** You're supposed to be busy and successful, remember? No one wants to do business with someone seen as needy. When setting a meeting time with a prospect, don't ignore your calendar and say, "Anytime next week is fine." You give the impression that you have no other work. Instead, make it a point to get out your calendar and say, "I am free to meet with you on Monday from one until three or Thursday between nine and eleven. Which fits your schedule?"

◆ **Prequalify potential clients.** Ask them if they are in a position to make purchasing decisions for your products or contract your services if you can demonstrate a workable and cost-efficient way to help them. The prospect will respect your concern for your own time, too.

◆ **Have up-to-date business cards available.** Never hand out cards with crossed-out information. Large companies can generally secure updated cards very quickly because many companies have in-house printing departments. Don't make yourself look small by using outdated cards.

◆ **Build rapport with your prospects.** Learn their personalities, then adapt your own behavior to increase compatibility. But heed this warning: Do not be a lapdog business owner; instead, display a slight air of indifference. Of course, you must show enthusiasm for your business and for what you do, but balance that against being perceived as overly eager to get an assignment or a sale. It's difficult to appear somewhat indifferent when you're really not, but you will be more desirable to prospects when they think they need you more than you need them. Entrepreneurs who are too available, too flexible, too bending, and too anxious rarely get the business, because they look too desperate. Do business on your terms, but make sure that your business practices and prices are reasonable and in line with the competition.

◆ **Remember to sell benefit and value, not just features.** In the first meeting, devote 80 percent of the time to what the client needs to eliminate company problems or to improve functions and only 20 percent of the time to explain your services and products. Be sure to discuss these points even if they're not specifically asked about:

—What services or products you provide

—What benefits your product offers

—How the company will profit from your services

—How the contact, the representative of the company, will profit from your services (you'll make their workload lighter, easier, and so on)

—What it will be like to work with you

—When these profits and benefits will be realized

—What guarantees, follow-up, or maintenance services you provide

◆ **Learn how to be interested instead of just being interesting.** Listen more and talk less. This was a lesson learned by Jeff Hopmayer, founder of Original American Scones, in Oak Park, Illinois, which last year sold $15 million worth of baked goods. "I tend to talk without listening, and big companies want you to listen first," Jeff says. "The more I pushed my products and my agenda with larger companies, the slower things went. One company spent $187,000 on focus groups to tell me it was OK to buy and sell my scones. That drove me nuts." This now-enlightened entrepreneur says he didn't land sales until "I realized that by listening I could more closely relate to my clients and what they wanted. The result? More sales." Jeff has since sold the company to Havi Food Services.

◆ **Be positive.** Business is always "good." If it is great, then say it is "Great!" However, a word of caution: Being proud of your success is deserved, but don't overdo it. Successful people are often the most understated. If business is lousy, then you are "very busy." After all, if business is lousy, you'd *better* be busy—busy marketing for more work!

◆ **Use plural references if possible.** Refer to your company as *us, we,* or *our,* not *I* or *my.* When discussing administrative or other minor tasks with a client, never say, "I will do this." Instead say, "I'll have this done" or "We'll take care of it."

◆ **Don't swear.** If you think that curse words or off-color expressions add emphasis to what you have to say, you're right, they do. They emphasize that you are uncultivated. One of my high school English teachers used to say that "Profanity is the audible expression of ignorance."

◆ **Promote the company more than yourself.** Employees affiliated with larger companies are expected to do this.

◆ **Maintain your integrity.** Don't compromise your fees, your advice, or your principles for any prospect or client. It's OK to bargain to a certain extent, but do not accept a request for a reduction in your fee unless the prospect is willing to accept a reduction in the scope of work or the amount of products provided for that fee. The exception to this rule would be those times when you assign a reduction, such as when you advertise a loss leader. In this case, you're selling at a price that represents a loss for you but that is intended to draw (lead) customers into your store in the hope that they will make additional purchases.

◆ **Find out what you have in common with your prospect and refer to it.** The idea is to establish trust because: (1) we trust people who are most like us, and (2) we trust people we can agree with. Knowing that, remind prospects of your similarities. This puts the customer in an agreeable, yes-type mode and starts the momentum that leads to trust. Even saying, "It's a great day, isn't it?" or "This office looks as though you take advantage of all its space" will make customers begin to think, "If I say yes, I obviously agree, and if I agree, I probably can trust this situation."

However, as my friend Garrie points out, make sure you select "yes" items that you can support in conversation. He tells an amusing story of the time he was trying to market to an insurance broker. "I noticed a nautical theme in his office, so I asked him if he was a boater. To that he replied 'yes' and went on for ten minutes about his sailboat. I know nothing about sailboats, so I couldn't ask anything since I was too unknowledgeable to know what to ask. I was forced to listen while looking for a segue to talk about my company. None came. After a while he realized I knew nothing and awkwardly asked what I had to tell him. I did not get the business."

◆ **Be forthright.** If you know that your client can get certain services more efficiently or cost-effectively and there's a good chance of that fact coming out with a bit of research, then bring that information to the table. You may sacrifice this sale, but you'll build credibility. Do not be afraid to mention your competitors in a positive way, such as by giving a minor referral or reference. Your willingness to do this will make you appear secure and will make others look more insecure and territorial.

◆ **Don't play dumb.** If you are asked questions about the competition and you know the answer, share it in a professional manner. Your customers want to know they are buying goods or services from someone who stays informed and competitive.

◆ **Participate in group conversations.** Occasionally it's appropriate to discuss limited in-house information with clients, such as when you are out to lunch and it seems to be expected of everyone to share stories from work. However, remember that every comment you make provides insight into the internal workings of your company. Therefore, instead of referring to your headaches from completing business tax forms, for example, mention your accountant or your accounting department. Even your complaints should make your company sound large.

◆ **Never ignore anyone.** Sometimes in trying to make an impression on one person in a group, it's easy to disregard others. About a year ago, I was sitting in a hotel breakfast bar in Boston with a friend of mine who is the owner of several educational publications. A young man approached our table, nodded at me, and began to pitch a story idea to my friend that would involve his doing research on sports stars. His concept was to show America's youth how sports heroes change as they gain prominence. My friend noticed that I was completely ignored by this young man's monologue, and although it wasn't his fault, my friend apologized to me afterward. This gave me the chance to share a story with him about how during my early days as a reporter one of my first assignments was to interview a nervous, publicity-shy, novice Baltimore Oriole who was trying to promote milk, his first major endorsement. He was none other than the now-famous Cal Ripken. My friend and I had a good laugh, and unfortunately (and unintentionally), it was at the expense of the young man. He had dismissed me, assuming I wouldn't be able to help him achieve his goal.

◆ **Factor prices with thought.** When you calculate fees, always quote an odd number. Say the fee will be $7,465 rather than $7,500. This way your prices look carefully factored and competitive.

◆ **Let prospects know what action you want them to take.** This applies to phone sales and direct mail, too; people may be in doubt about what step to take next, so be sure to suggest something! For example, direct mail should tell them to "Complete the enclosed card and return it" or "Visit our Web site at www.thegoodguys.com." If you're meeting in person and have just convinced your prospect to purchase your services, try "Simply issue the purchase order by Friday and we can begin work on Monday." The point is to make it as easy as possible for the prospect to do business with you and to take the next step in making that happen. Even if you're not sure what the prospect is thinking, suggest an action: "I'll call you on Friday. Between now and then, call my references and get an idea of how easy it is to get this project started."

◆ **When you call after the meeting, don't ask for business or ask for a decision.** Doing so gives the impression that you are desperate. Instead, find a different but solid reason to communicate with them—new information, something in the paper that pertains to their situation or company—and use that as an introduction for your call.

◆ **Don't appear cheap.** Don't covet a client's office, office equipment, cars, home, and so on. Admiring and complimenting are OK; displaying excessive appreciation of a desirable item is inappropriate and signals jealousy. Further, don't ask a client for tablets, paper, pens, and so forth. Come with your own materials. If you worked for a big company, you'd have all the nice office equipment and supplies, too.

◆ **Don't waste time overexplaining, apologizing, or justifying your opinions.** It will undermine your confident and powerful image. Brief, factual statements delivered with confident body language are the most effective way to get the result you desire.

◆ **Talk about past successes, not specific clients.** Prospects
might assume that if you are talking about past clients now,
they will be the subject of discussions in the future.

◆ **Present a well-rounded person.** It's impressive to own
your own business; it's not quite as impressive if the business owns you. After you've established a relationship with a
client, don't talk about work all the time. A sign of success is
that you have a healthy balance of work and play. This is
especially true now. When I was at the peak of running my
company, I enjoyed collecting things and seeing what my
money could buy. Now, like many other people I'm meeting,
I'm more interested in collecting experiences than things.
Experiences make you a more interesting and well-rounded
person and keep your mind sharp and balanced for returning to work when you're ready.

◆ **Don't be a blabbermouth.** Use silence effectively. You don't
want your clients to think that you never get out or that you
never have anyone to talk to. Many home-based businesses
fail because the owners get tired of the solo act. We all need
to share exciting news when business is good and hear a pep
talk when business is poor. We also need to talk to others to
humanize our work, connect to peers, and validate our perspective on issues. However, never turn to a client for any of
this support; instead, find a support group, a spouse, or a
friend to talk to.

When you decide to ignore the aforementioned guideline
and share successes or complaints, make sure they are all
company-related and all designed to make your company
look better and successful. Talking about your nanny, housekeeper, cook, personal trainer, investment counselor, prestigious car, or lavish vacation to someone who might not be
able to afford them is classless and rude.

In addition to those topics, avoid the following subjects
with all clients (and most colleagues, too):

—salaries (yours *and* your spouse's)

—major investments

—bankruptcies and other financial problems

—details of a divorce

—illicit affairs

—secrets about a client's employees

—extreme or detailed views on religion and politics

—client confidences, complaints, and plans

—closely held company product information (yours or the client's), like the actual cost of the raw materials for a best-selling product

—insults about the competition

—sales figures (in some instances)

—price breaks you granted to someone else

—new products that have not yet been introduced

—articles or books that have not yet been published

—medical payments, coverage, or bills

And finally, never, never, *never* make a remark that possibly could be perceived as:

—racist

—sexist

—off-color

—insulting

—offensive

—dishonorable

—suggestive of anything but business

The last thing you want is a discrimination or harassment lawsuit filed against you. Even if a lawsuit is not filed, your image will suffer from improper comments or behavior.

Work to communicate at every level. With a client base ranging from the famous to the totally obscure, I have developed the ability to show everyone respect and have learned to relate to each client in the way that best meets individual needs. Besides, today's low-profile client could be tomorrow's famous client.

What Should You Wear When You Meet with Clients?

IN THIS DAY OF CASUAL BUSINESS ATTIRE, IT'S HARD TO KNOW how to dress for any office situation. Fortunately, it's quite appropriate to ask your prospects about the business attire at their offices. If you can't do that, then the best rule is to dress one step better than how you think your client will dress. If you don't know, err on the side of being more formal. My friend Garrie errs on the side of business formality because he wants to show his clients respect. "I buy thousand-dollar suits because I can, and it makes me feel successful," he says. "Furthermore, I buy Bally shoes because they are comfortable, and they look like they cost $400. Don't let anyone kid you. People who wear expensive clothes, such as conservative suits, may hear derisive comments from time to time, but these clothes make you feel successful and look successful, and people buy from winners." Garrie must know what works for him; he built his telecommunications company to more than 10,000 customers within seven years.

In contrast, my friend Jay Massey has been known to wear flip-flops and shorts to business meetings. "We break all the rules for what a successful marketing firm should be," says Jay, the president and main client contact of Coco Design Associates in Pensacola, Florida. "I don't try to impress a new client with an expensive suit and a Rolex watch. I just try to be myself. I know if they hire my firm it's because they like what's in my head, comes out of my mouth, or is displayed in our portfolio."

Perhaps Jay can say this because he's in a creative field or because he lives in Florida, whereas Garrie is in telecommunications and lives in Boston. Your line of work and geographic location do make a difference. However, if you're still unsure, err on the side of conservative dress. When it comes to buying business clothing and coats, the best rule of thumb is still to stick with executive colors. You can't go wrong with camel, navy, black, or gray.

Carry Quality Accessories

BESIDES THE PERSONAL TRAITS YOU CARRY WITH YOU INTO every meeting—enthusiasm, intelligence, persistence, patience, confidence, humor, and warmth—it also helps to carry the right stuff (or toys, as most entrepreneurs call them). Does your umbrella have holes? Does your raincoat look like Detective Columbo's? If so, it's time to replace them. Each item you use, carry, or drive prompts impressions about your age, nationality, socioeconomic level, job status, familiarity and comfort with current technology, taste, and judgment—which, in turn, are a reflection of your company.

Scrutinize what shows when your briefcase is open. Keep your accessories in good shape and up-to-date, too. Make sure your case does not carry things like a brown-paper-bagged lunch, deodorant, breath spray, any nonbusiness-related literature, offensive materials, or books entitled *How to Impress Your Client.*

Apply to all frequent flier programs if the nature of your business suggests clients nationwide or internationally. Fill your briefcase cardholders with them so that they show whenever your briefcase is open. I bought a stitched-leather card case to hold all my hotel and frequent flier cards for less than $80, yet it looks like one costing several times that.

If you are in the habit of opening your day planner in front of clients, make sure that you have penciled in (in your own code) lots of entries that will make you look as busy as you in fact are. To distinguish what's actual business from what is not, use different colors of ink or a routine marking for nonbusiness notations. For example, add a 1 or some other distinguishable mark for personal notes; appointments will not bear this designation.

Get a credit card with your company name on it, prefer-ably a gold or platinum card. The implication with a gold card is that you are successful enough to afford one; most professional people are aware that some prestige cards charge a higher-than-usual annual fee and that the balance must be paid off each month.

Some people use affinity credit cards that have other com-pany's names on them, from Northwest Airlines to the Balti-more Orioles. If you use one, make sure that the name is prestigious or pertinent to you and your work.

Carry a *nice* pen. After my second Montblanc pen disap-peared, I switched to a cheaper Guilloche. That and a tablet were soon lost on the highways of Maryland after I left them on the roof of my car. It was then that I stopped seeing pens as status symbols and began regarding them as a bothersome expense, because you shouldn't use a cheap one. A Bic generally doesn't make the same statement that an all-silver or gold pen does. However, even the standard Cross pen looks elegant.

I remember when laptop computers were first available at a reasonable price. I was doing a lot of client visits in those days and thus a lot of flying. It wasn't long before these toys became symbols of success, and I'd see them hauled out and fired up the moment the pilot gave the word that all was clear. But, of course, that phase passed, and it soon became more trendy if you *didn't* have to carry a laptop. It implied that you were so successful you weren't tied to a machine, or that you had a large staff doing work for you. I had purchased one so that I could take it along on business trips and do work on the road. However, it became very annoying to carry a purse, a briefcase, and a laptop computer, and I realized that I felt more like a loaded pack mule than an organized executive. I finally left the laptop at home.

Wear conservative amounts of nice jewelry. I was surprised that an article in *Working Woman* magazine (p. 54, March 1999) gave this advice about watches: If you "worry that people will notice you're wearing an impostor (as opposed to a genuine Rolex or other expensive watch), visit a thrift shop and buy a man's vintage watch. To anyone nervy enough to ask, refer to it as a 'timepiece' and tell people it belonged to Daddy, thereby giving it immense sentimental value." I agree that your watch, as with everything you wear or carry, should be of quality, and I think it's clever to buy a man's watch at a thrift shop; however, I don't think you should ever lie about it. Instead, just agree that it's unique and move on.

Use a writing tablet in a leather holder or binder with the company name imprinted or embossed on it. The impression it makes: how lucky you are that your company is large and successful enough to hand out such nice items to its employees.

Don't take medicines in front of clients. Although you know that you are popping an innocent aspirin for the headache brought on by your client's incessant talking, it's only human nature to assume the worst: your client may think you're taking pills for a bad heart or an ulcer. The logical next thought will be: "Will this guy be around tomorrow to handle my business?"

Don't drive a beater car. If you can't afford a nice car, then always park where a client cannot see it. If possible, personalize your plate. My friend Jim Morrison, of James N. Morrison & Associates in Green Bay, speaks professionally and teaches presentation and leadership skills; his plate reads "ISPK4U."

EXPECT THE UNEXPECTED

PREPARING IN ADVANCE TO
SAFEGUARD YOUR IMAGE

CAN YOU HANDLE UNEXPECTED SITUATIONS? ADAPT TO CONtinually changing rules? Work with people of varying experiences and positions?

The world seems to be moving from being logical and rational to being unpredictable and creatively chaotic. And nowhere is this more prevalent than in the world of business. Today's new economy is filled with start-ups, acquisitions, turnarounds, reengineered organizations, mergers, de-mergers, new regulatory climates, and litigious uncertainty. The Internet is revolutionizing ways of conducting business even as you read this book. As a small business owner who wants to thrive in this environment, you will have to learn how to deal with and adapt to constantly changing situations. This section should help you.

When it comes to survival, a small business needs to adapt constantly to demands in the marketplace. However, when it comes to basic philosophy and beliefs, a small business is well served to set its standards and stick with them. How do you know when to change and when to stand firm? Let's take a look at several areas individually:

◆ **Establish and enforce credit policies.** Poor credit practices cost small businesses millions of dollars per year because owners determine their policies in a seat-of-the-pants style. If you want to compete with big companies, then do what they have been doing for years: be fair but tough with credit; that is, determine how much risk you are willing to take, set fair rules, then be tough in protecting and obeying them in every situation. One owner of a wedding consulting service was so accustomed to operating informally on personal instincts that she let this carry over into lending credit, too. "I learned the hard way," she says. "I was hired to do a large job for a friend of a friend. Because of our mutual acquaintance, I didn't bother to check her credit. Two years after the wedding, I still had collected only 60 percent of the bill. Add to that, I had turned down another wedding for that same day for a couple whose oldest daughter was getting married. Within that same year, her two sisters got married, too! They used the same consultant for all three weddings." The bottom line is that it does no good to make a big sale if you don't get paid for it.

However, you should offer at least one form of credit—be it credit cards or an extended payment plan. Otherwise, you will risk losing a significant percentage of potential customers to the competition. It is possible to maximize the benefits of business credit while reducing the risks; all it takes is a strict and uniform system of credit screening for *all* customers. It would be impossible for me to suggest policies here; your credit and screening practices will be determined by your product or service, your location, your clientele, and your competition's policies. Your best bet is to find out what other companies in your field have done, especially your competition, and then establish your policies.

Be sure to protect yourself by stating your credit terms clearly on your invoices. If you do make a mistake in lending credit, don't become your own collection agency. Let a professional collection agency handle the concern of bad debt. Agencies are well prepared to deal with the cagey routines of delinquent accounts.

◆ **Use letters of agreement and contracts.** In addition to having your credit terms spelled out, put every business transaction in writing. Be so specific that the client's obligations are spelled out, too, including timely payment of invoices and provision of working space, documents, administrative support, and access to personnel. The benefits of doing this are many: it promotes your image as an experienced business, explains your terms and agreements (which helps to eliminate the risk of misunderstanding), and gives you documentation for proof if you ever have to resolve a dispute or disagreement.

◆ **Know your insurance needs.** Most standard home owner's policies are not comprehensive enough for a home-based business. Make a list of your inventory, then meet with a business insurance agent to make sure your equipment and supplies are protected. You may also need liability coverage for both your office and your products and services; income replacement coverage, in case some sort of unexpected situation keeps you from working for any significant length of time; errors and omissions insurance in case a client takes exception to your advice; and disability insurance. And if you have a partner, consider purchasing insurance on each other to ensure financial security in the event of untimely death.

◆ **Practice for crucial first contacts with customers.** Just as in social relationships, if you turn off a person at the first encounter in business, then that's the image they're likely to carry from that day on. Don't open your doors for business until you've practiced dealing with customers. Sound corny? Perhaps, but take a lesson from musicians and actors: practice in private before presenting your act to the public. All the kinks and wrinkles should be ironed out before the opening ribbon is cut. If you have a storefront, spend at least two full days prior to opening to rehearse every aspect of the company's operations, duplicating all the intricacies of an actual business day. I recommend two days, because if all goes well, then you should practice again the day before opening. If things don't go well, you have another day to work on the problem areas. Employees should pose as customers. Have them buy merchandise, ask for advice or assistance, and make complaints. Here's a checklist to review before opening your doors:

—Know who will cope with customer complaints and how they will be handled

—Put your equipment through every conceivable use that will be required during opening day

—Have at least 20 percent more inventory than you think you will need

—Present your staff with "what if" scenarios and have them describe—or better still, walk through—how they will handle each situation

—Discuss with the staff how they will deal with problems such as the fire alarm sounding, a customer caught stealing, or an uncontrolled child who begins to damage merchandise

—Make sure the place shines. Do not open your doors until the store or office is completely finished. You want your customers to know from the very first visit what they can expect on future visits

—Practice, practice, practice

◆ **Protect your company secrets.** Shred unnecessary documents containing company secrets. Of course, you should secure and file originals, but shred copies of sensitive documents like contracts, profit and loss statements, invoices and sales reports, customer lists, and passwords.

◆ **Know your market.** It may be time to update your perspective on your business. No matter how well you defined your market in your business plan when you started, it's unlikely to remain static. This means you will have to revisit your business plan each year. If you don't stay abreast of changes in your market, you can't respond in competitive ways. Additionally, with your growth, you may be able to serve more (or different) markets than what you handled before. This could change the entire focus of your business.

The bad news is that this research will take some time. The good news is that you don't have to do it all yourself. If you're short on time, consider hiring someone to do it for you. A variety of "infopreneurs" are available to assist you, selling everything from high-level market research to demographic and psychographic information on your potential customers to elaborate and detailed mailing lists. What you want to find out are the changing dynamics that affect your company.

If you're completely strapped for cash and can't afford infopreneurs, then schedule some affordable counseling at a Small Business Development Center. There are more than 1,000 centers around the country, jointly funded by the U.S. Small Business Administration (SBA) and private organizations, usually colleges or universities. Find one near you by calling your local SBA. They're listed in the blue pages in the telephone directory under "United States government."

◆ **Stay abreast of changes.** In the past several years, the Internet has been the most prevalent entity changing the way we do business. To those who adopted this tool early, it has delivered impressive results through millions of electronic customers, unlimited online revenues, and incredible market capitalization. Unfortunately, there are still many industries that have not learned how to make the Internet work to their advantage, and I predict many small business professionals— such as insurance agents, travel agents, car dealers, booksellers, and drugstore owners and pharmacists—are going to have to adapt to the changing ways of doing business over the Net or they will be looking at uncertain futures. Last year, a *U.S. News & World Report* magazine cover story said that due to the Internet, "childhood, work, romance, and old age will never be the same." How, then, can anyone be blind to its impact on and benefit to small businesses? Already the Internet has broken down the traditional boundaries and limitations between buyers and sellers, helped launch thousands of new businesses, and created hundreds of jobs that as little as ten years ago did not exist. For example, I've been contacted many times to provide an online article or report, and I have several friends who are online freelance writers. One of them uses a "virtual" assistant. Take note, however, that even though this same *U.S. News & World Report* article said that 2.2 billion e-mail messages are sent each day, these messages are just words— bare words. Your intonation, impressive handshake and smile, facial expressions, and any in-person traits you use to impress clients cannot be sent via e-mail. Bottom line: Continue to meet clients in person as you use the Internet and e-mail to your business advantage.

Markets shift and grow in other ways besides through the Internet. I'm proud that years ago I anticipated both regulatory changes and tightening budgets in the nuclear industry. I had built a solid business servicing commercial nuclear power plants, which are required by the federal government to have crisis management plans in place. When I spotted our market changing, my company—unlike our prime competitors—studied other industries, became proficient in their regulations, began to network and market in their circles, and soon had shifted the majority of our work away from nuclear plants to companies in the chemical, airline, department store, banking, and manufacturing fields. With that experience, our expansion into still more industries was a simple progression, and soon we had contracts with NASA and UPS. At least three of our competitors did not identify or adapt to the changes, and they eventually closed their doors.

Compare my story with one my friend Jim Morrison tells about a professional speaker friend who planned an entire year's worth of income through one company: "He was booked for about fifty programs over the course of about twelve months with a well-known, large manufacturing company that had offices in several cities. He was to do three to five presentations at each location to cover all employees. The speaker is a sole proprietor and did not have a kill fee, because he had worked for that company on many occasions and had no reason to doubt the bookings. Suddenly he got a call that his services were not needed; the company was cutting back due to talks of a potential takeover. He had to scramble to fill his calendar that year as best he could. He no longer puts all his eggs in one basket."

Sometimes your market might not change at all, especially if you have a monopoly on it. Pat Merenko Smith, president of Revelation Productions in North Huntingdon, Pennsylvania, noted that change in her company was due anyway to satisfy her customers. She tells the story of her business and her adaptations to meet customers' needs: "My whole business was based on providing something that people wanted but could not find anywhere, and I knew that was a fact because I was someone who needed such materials. I taught a Bible class at our church on the book of Revelation, a book that is filled with descriptions of symbolic visions. When I couldn't find visuals to supplement my own teaching, I did them myself. I filled the void by producing an original series of art fifteen years ago. Although I still have no competition, I seek suggestions from my customers for new products that they may need as technology changes. For example, when we first started out, people wanted 35mm slides for teaching to large groups, then as years went by I got more and more requests for overhead transparencies. Now I am getting requests to have all my artwork available on CD-ROM for PowerPoint presentations."

◆ **Make it easy for people to do business with you.** If you've noticed a downswing in customer patronage, you may have inadvertently set up roadblocks to doing business. Determine how easy it is for your customers to work with you, as compared to your competition:

—Do you have convenient hours? Not everyone works 9-to-5 every day.

—Would offering free delivery set you apart from the competition?

—Do you miss enough phone calls throughout the day that it would be better for you to rearrange your schedule?

—Would you double your orders if you had a toll-free number?

—Are you flexible? When your customers ask for something out of the ordinary, do you consider their requests? Remember, if you don't, your bigger competition probably eventually will.

◆ **Pay attention to sales.** I've said elsewhere in this book that if you're operating your own business, then you're involved in sales whether you want to be or not. Sometimes, despite your best efforts and convincing yourself that you've finally got the knack of this selling thing, you will experience a sales slump. Nothing you do will seem to work. And, in fact, the more you try, the worse things get. The key is to deal with it, not dwell on it. You have to determine whether you're truly experiencing a temporary slump or whether sales have taken a downturn due to seasonal reasons or changes in your market. To decide, look at all the possible factors that may be contributing to the downturn:

—Have you cut down on the number of sales calls you're making, whether in person or over the phone?

—Are you treating your current customers with the respect they deserve?

—If your product comes with a guarantee, are you honoring that guarantee? If your service is supposed to produce certain results, is it fulfilling its promise?

—Are you focusing on newer and perhaps more lucrative prospects at the expense of current customers?

—Has there been a turn in the economy?

—Has a new competitor opened in the same market?

—Has an existing competitor changed its policies?

—How do this year's sales compare to last year's? If there was a similar drop at the same time last year, it may be a seasonal quirk. If there was no drop, then what's different between last year and this year?

—Has a major customer moved out of the area? Or has it expanded its in-house services, thus eliminating the need for your help?

—Have you changed the quality of your product or service?

—Have you changed delivery services or routines?

—Have you cut back on marketing?

Next it's time to look at yourself. Perhaps you've become stale because you've been doing things the same way for too long. Perhaps it's time to emphasize a different benefit of your service so that customers hear something new. I did this with my crisis management firm. For years, I had been expounding the virtues of being prepared for the worst-case scenario. I began to bore not only my customers but myself as well. So I did an assessment of how my services were benefiting companies in other, more bottom-line ways. For example, it was common for companies to reengineer their routines for certain business functions as a result of seeing those functions operate during simulated crisis situations. Inevitably, when I put a company through a mock scenario in which they were required to respond as realistically as possible, they would discover that the procedures I had set up for making purchases, securing travel, or collecting vital information were streamlined in comparison to their outdated, heavily staff-dependent, time-consuming methods. So I began to share with potential clients how other companies were able to make changes that improved their bottom line and their day-to-day activities by developing crisis response plans. My prospects soon began to see that developing plans for crisis times meant cleaning house and cutting the fat from their business functions—something most of them felt it was necessary to do anyway. Thus, with our services, not only did clients get an excellent program for responding to emergencies, but they also received enough information and support from our meetings and reports to begin establishing the foundation for necessary changes.

Client Questions That Affect the Image of Home-based and Small Business Entrepreneurs

THERE'S NOTHING AS AWKWARD AS UNEXPECTEDLY BEING asked a question whose answer could prove embarrassing or too revealing of you and your company's size, age, success, or standing. The best way to deal with these unexpected questions is to be prepared for them. But if they're unexpected, how can you prepare?

Below is a list of twenty-five questions affecting image that are frequently asked of small business owners. Prepare your clever, insightful, and not-too-revealing answers now so that you can deliver them in an extemporaneous manner when necessary. Be sure to review them with partners and key company personnel to make sure you all are delivering the same message. For some of the tougher or more potentially damaging questions, I have provided guidance or suggestions.

1 How are you? Was the trip good? Did you have trouble finding us? You are terrific, the trip was pleasant, and you had no trouble finding them. That's because you're always positive, you enjoy every aspect of your work, and you take the time to get directions in advance. Don't let anything negative enter into your conversation. Keep everything positive, even the basics of finding your client despite a congested city, an early morning flat tire, and three wrong turns.

2 **How long has your company been in business?** If the answer is only a short time, then expound on how much experience you gained in the field prior to launching the business.

3 **Do you publish an annual report?** "We're required to publish only X, but I can provide you with some written materials describing our business."

4 **How are you different from your competition?** Elaborate on your positive qualities, not the competitor's negative qualities.

5 **How are your products or services different from the competition?** This will have to be uniquely your answer.

6 **How will you improve on the service we have with our current vendor?** Know your competition and have your answer ready!

7 **How many employees do you have?** "Fortunately we are small, which will be to your benefit. You see, our competitors are larger; they have more employees. We prefer to work with associates on an as-needed basis. This way, rather than assigning an employee who isn't specifically qualified to do the job you need accomplished—as our competition must do to ensure their people are billable—we can pick and choose from a long list of associates, selecting the professional most qualified to do your job. We do this so that you'll be satisfied and turn to us again."

8 **How large is your company?** You don't have to give numbers. Instead say, "Large enough to handle this project with the best people on staff," or something else true but equally noncommittal. Then move on to add, "My contacts for this job range from . . ." or "My vendors know that I expect. . .." thus giving your client the assurance that he's actually seeking.

9 **How many people work for you?** When someone asks this, you could laughingly answer, "About half of them," then quickly change the subject. (A word of caution: evaluate each situation before using this technique—sparingly. Your words

could imply that you're not happy with your staff or that the staff is lazy.) When you must provide the information, instead of just saying "five," try this:

Them: "So, how many people work for you?"

You: "Well, given that we are open six days a week, can turn around orders within a day, have the latest in equipment and a client base of more than seventy-five satisfied customers, how big do you think we are?"

Them: "Oh, I don't know. . . twenty?"

You (very proudly): "Five! Isn't that great?"

10 Where is your store/office/headquarters located? It's OK to give your home address and move on, if your home address is a business-friendly one. (See "If You Work from Home," page 28, for details on business addresses.)

11 What justifies your higher cost? You alone know this answer. Make it convincing and worthwhile.

12 Who is using your products in the same way that we plan to use them? If the answer is no one, be up front about it. Say something like this: "No one. This is an opportunity for you to be a leader. This means that use of this product will establish you as an innovative thinker and may even bring you publicity by the local press or others in your industry."

13 Who are your primary customers, and how do you meet their requirements? Again, your answer.

14 What kind of customer service can I expect? Ditto.

15 What products or services do you plan on introducing in the near future? Here's your chance to educate your client about what services you provide; and because you've done your homework and have a good idea what his needs are, you can share that you're considering launching a product or service that you know will pique his interest.

16 Do you maintain local inventory? or **What lead times are required?** Your answer.

17 Can you deliver on time? How much do I have to order to receive daily delivery? Your answer.

18 Do you offer quantity discounts? Do you have a lower-priced similar product? Your answer.

19 How did you gain your expertise? Your answer.

20 How will your service improve my profitability? Your answer.

21 Have you done innovative things (inaugurated new systems, developed new procedures) for other companies? Of course you have! You have developed very good solutions to other clients' problems. Due to confidentiality agreements, you can't share their names, but you'd be happy to share the problems and solutions.

22 How is your company organized? You can't say, "Well, my company has five levels, and I'm all five of them." Instead say, "I'm in charge, so if you have problems, you'll be working directly with me." Then quickly move on.

23 What do you think of XYZ's (your competitor's) products or services? You may not think much of them, but you don't say that. Instead say, "XYZ and I have a friendly association, and I admire their (choose something innocuous); however, for specifics about their company, you should probably talk to them. I can tell you that we differ in that we. . . (expound heartily on your own virtues)."

24 What are your company's plans for growth and expansion? Make them good!

25 If you own your own business, you must be rich. Are you? "I have a very satisfying life and thoroughly enjoy the work I do." Then move on.

Know How to Find Strength When Hit with Adversity

MOST PEOPLE AGREE THAT ADVERSITY BUILDS CHARACTER, BUT many would doubt that adversity is good for building a small business. Ann King, however, would argue otherwise. As CEO of the Atlanta-based gourmet gift service Blooming Cookies Catalog Company, Ann experienced a start-up that was plagued by a series of hardships, any one of which would have sent many entrepreneurs packing. Her motto for survival? "Be yourself and believe in what you're doing. I believe that everything happens for a reason," Ann says. "Remember that, when you're dealing with the established competition."

Most people who experienced what Ann did would have a hard time understanding the reasons behind these setbacks: dishonest real estate agents, a banker who dispensed the wrong advice, arson, theft, disastrous alliances, sudden and unexpected huge debt, and inexperience that cost $20,000 on one deal alone.

In one tragic incident, she and her partner, Ashley Ghegan, watched as firefighters battled their burning building for four hours. After the fire, Ann says she and her partner began to focus more on marketing rather than "trying to spread ourselves too thin. The fire really affected the way we did business. We were underinsured, so we didn't have the ability to structure ourselves the way we were before."

Following the fire, a local news station reported that Blooming Cookies had burned down. Ann immediately called the station and announced they would be open for business on Monday morning. When that story ran, Ann says, "Everyone called in and placed orders to help support us." As a result, on their first day back in operation they filled more than $5,000 in orders—the biggest day in their history at that point.

Today, with 60,000 customers, international distribution, sales reaching $3.5 million, and an impressive Internet partnership with Kodak, Ann believes it was her inner strength that helped her through all her ordeals.

The moral of the story: If you believe in what you're doing, stick with it. Know where you can find strength and help—physical, financial, mental, spiritual—when adversity does hit.

CHAPTER 2

Involving Other People in Your Plans

GO SOLO, BUT NOT ALONE

PROJECTING A BIG IMAGE
WITHOUT HIRING EMPLOYEES

O SURVIVE——OR TRIUMPH!——AS AN ENTREPRE-
neur, you have to have multiple personalities,
because you are responsible for every aspect of your
business. You've already laughed with your family
about the many hats you wear, from receptionist to
CEO, from janitor to director of sales. Eventually,
though, competing with big organizations takes
more than a juggling of roles; it takes the *perception*
of size, which implies a need for you to actually
grow (with a staff or partners) or to *become* many
people on your own.

You have options, of course, from faking your
size with the help of marketing materials and office
equipment to taking on business partners to hiring

employees. The next section, "Harness Well-Meaning Family and Employees" on page 90, will discuss growth through hiring employees. But first let's talk about entrepreneurs who do not want to take on the burden of a staff. There are several ways to turn your business into an operation of "many" people without hiring employees:

- use business cards creatively
- form an advisory board
- link up with a business support network
- secure a mentor
- form a partnering arrangement with another entrepreneur or company in a related line of work
- find a partner
- work with a virtual partner
- consider outsourcing
- look for an angel

Use Business Cards Creatively

IF YOU DON'T THINK A COMPANY PRESIDENT IN YOUR LINE
of work should make sales calls, then print separate business
cards that announce you to be Director of Sales or Vice President of Marketing. After all, you *are* those roles, too, right? A
word of caution: think this process through completely. If at
any point you have to meet with clients as company president, then your credibility may be tarnished. Clients might
assume you were trying to mislead them. I have met entrepreneurs who were willing to take this gamble, however.
They were so positive they could deliver knock-your-socks-off
service that they believed clients would be amused by their
approach in the end. And in many cases, it worked.

Form an Advisory Board

BESIDES OFFERING YOU GOOD ADVICE AND AN OBJECTIVE
opinion, a board of advisers can heighten your image. Sometimes just printing the names of advisory board members on
company literature can imply size, success, and stability. And
because you select them, you can request that your advisers
do as little or as much with the company as you want. If you
don't want their advice, don't ask; but be sure to list them in
your marketing material and letterhead nevertheless.

A board of advisers gives you credibility. If you want to
compete with major corporations—which offer layers of
impressive names and titles—you'll want to align yourself
with some impressive names and titles, too. If your advisers
are well respected, you will receive respect based on your
affiliation with them.

Therefore, advisers should be people who are well
regarded by the business community and who believe in
you and your company. The better known and more experienced your advisers are, the better your credibility will be.
In situations where your ability or experience might be
questioned, you can draw attention to your board of advisers. So be crafty when selecting them. What corporate executives, association leaders, entrepreneurs, or government

officials are held in high esteem in your field? In your town or region? What well-known business trainers, authors, hosts of TV or radio business programs, and retired executives do you know? Create your advisory board with these people in mind.

Peggy Isaacson had very clear ideas of whom she wanted when she formed an advisory board for her human resources management firm, Florida-based Peggy Isaacson & Associates. "Several years ago I was experiencing a motivation slump and felt I needed to have some sort of entity to which I would be accountable for doing what I needed to do for the business," Peggy explains. "I needed to get fresh ideas for the business and to have what I call a watercooler crowd." She sought people whose judgment and opinions she trusted and respected and in front of whom she could be "less than perfect, without fear of criticism or ridicule." She also looked for expertise that would be useful to her. "I chose a client who is also a human resources professional, to represent the client's point of view and to understand the nature of the work I do; an accountant, to represent fiscal wisdom and who understood the needs and problems of small businesses; and a professional writer, who I knew had a good understanding of marketing as well as knowledge of small businesses." Peggy says they originally met about once a month but now meet with some regularity in the third and fourth quarter of each year.

Peggy says the board's relationship has been beneficial to everyone involved. "Except for the client, we're all home-based, so not only do they help me, but everyone has a lot to offer each other." She credits the board with preventing her from making some big mistakes and with keeping her on track. "Sometimes you just need an objective outside opinion to help you see what you can't see yourself," she says.

It's a good idea to offer to pay your board of advisers and to cover their travel expenses if you bring them together. I have served on two advisory boards in the past couple of years. One of the companies had sixty-two employees, and the owner could afford a generous payment for his board members. The other company, however, was a three-person organization, and the offer of $500 a year was fine with me, because I thoroughly believed in the company's mission, products, and management.

Of course, if you're smart, you will stay in contact with your advisers between meetings, too, since you've taken care to select them from the best available. With this mix of experts, you can ensure that your company will always benefit from a variety of opinions and skills. Other—and sometimes more important!—benefits of an advisory board are that through them you may build strong alliances that you otherwise might never have secured, and you may gain access to needed capital.

A word of caution: Don't confuse a board of advisers with a board of directors. The difference is significant. A board of advisers is an informal group of people who dispense advice and counsel a business without assuming any legal or financial responsibilities. A board of directors is a legal entity whose members have fiscal responsibility and are sometimes given partial ownership (or shares) in return for their participation. A board of directors is required for nonprofits, corporations, and public companies. Boards of directors can be held liable should the company become involved in litigation.

Link Up with a Business Support Network

A BUSINESS NETWORKING GROUP IS LIKE A BOARD OF ADVISERS who have businesses that are noncompetitive. These professionals serve as an excellent resource, brain trust, and support system for one another.

Denise Richards, owner of Aspen Communications, founded the Home Business Alliance in Irvine, California, because she had started a home-based business and "didn't know much about running it. I wanted to get together with other home-based businesses so we could figure it out together." The Alliance includes some graphic designers and a photographer, copywriter, list broker, interior designer, awards and screen-printing service owner, financial planner, business consultant, Web designer, and marketing consultant. Members promote one another. "I hate to use the term support group," Denise laughs, "but that's kind of how it works. The Alliance provides the chance to bounce around marketing ideas, exchange resources, or just vent frustrations. And I can build business relationships on a friendly basis. I can be honest with them and let them know when something isn't going right or I need more clients. At those times, everyone pitches in to help think of ideas; whereas at other networking groups, when your goal is to win business, you can't always be honest and admit that you're in a slump."

Secure a Mentor

IF YOU DON'T WANT TO TAKE ON A BOARD OF ADVISERS BUT like the idea of having at least one person who will look over your shoulder and steer you in the right direction, then find a mentor.

In my experience, finding a mentor is akin to finding love. When you go looking, you rarely find it. Mentors seem to evolve, or turn up, when you're not looking. They are people you slowly come to trust and respect, people who talk to you about your company and ask you questions. Before long they feel comfortable enough to dispense friendly advice, and the next thing you know, you're turning to them for insights into how to operate your business. Generally, not until long after they've played the role will you realize that they are, indeed, your mentors. This realization usually sets in after you become aware that you've willingly accepted negative feedback from them for something you've done.

Mentors are valuable, irreplaceable people for many reasons, the first being that they help you because they want to. They call you friend; you call them mentor and friend.

Mentors can generally provide personal introductions, critical feedback, insights into your field, and basic business knowledge. They tend to be older and thus have experience to offer so that you don't have to waste years collecting the same experience. Because you turned to someone you respected, chances are they were once "somebody" in your industry, which means they still may have valuable contacts. Even your larger competitors may not have those contacts.

Several mentors have played important roles in my life, especially in my professional life as a journalist and entrepreneur. I've always been lucky to find people who have accomplished the same things I want to accomplish and people who are particularly satisfied and confident. I found my mentors simply by making contact, either through a note, a formal letter introducing myself, or a telephone call. I never, however, mentioned the word "mentor" until they had already begun filling that role.

Form a Partnering Arrangement

ONE WAY OF APPEARING BIGGER AND RICHER THAN YOU ARE is to widen your prospect base; however, that can be a daunting challenge if you're already stretched in time and resources. Instead of trying to do it alone or adding overhead, forge a partnership with companies and specialists who offer complementary services. Building relationships with other businesses increases sales for all. Having a partner lets you create a big-company image while sharing marketing chores and miscellaneous expenses.

Beyond the cost savings, you'll also gain access to valuable resources, such as prospect lists. I've seen freelance writers, graphic designers, and public relations specialists team up to offer full-service marketing and publication services. I once helped a landscaping service increase revenue by 40 percent in six months through an alliance with a nursery. Another advantage: they both reduced their amount of marketing time.

You could also join with a partner to launch a new product or service. If you work with a major association or company that already markets to the same target audience as yours, you may be able to launch the product nationally and save thousands of dollars in the process. For example, while I was writing this book, I finished another, self-published book, *The Complete Home Improvement and Decorating Organizer*. Since it's a fill-in-the-entries type of journal and reference book, I insisted that it be sold in a quality three-ring binder; therefore, traditional publishing houses were not interested. A binder allows readers ease in writing and the option of adding as many personal papers, contracts, and manuals as they wish, but such binders cannot be distributed through bookstores or libraries. Although it's already available at Amazon.com, I am also pursuing partnerships with building supply companies, realtors, and mortgage firms. These organizations already have the audience, and because they work directly with home owners, I know they are interested in products that can promote their purpose.

Find a Partner

PARTNERS CAN BE THE BIGGEST BLESSING OR THE WORST nightmare for any entrepreneur, depending upon the arrangements and the relationship you share. Ideally, your partner will have skills and strengths in your weak areas. My former partner and I formed our company because we were so much alike, shared the same skills and goals, and approached work with like minds and practices. Unfortunately, that meant that while we were both strong in marketing and in project management, we were both woefully lacking when it came to legal and accounting issues, for example. While we were educating ourselves in these areas, we had to outsource the work, which cut into our bottom line. Had the two of us been strong in different areas, we would have saved immensely on our expenses.

So who would make a good partner? In my experience, friends, lovers, and spouses make the worst partners. If the company doesn't suffer from such an arrangement, then the personal relationship will. Sometimes, sadly, both will take a hit.

The best partner is someone with whom you have a history of working well—a person with whom you share common philosophies, likes and dislikes, goals, and work styles. The more experience you've had working together, the better. My former partner and I were friends long before we started our company together, so I was comfortable with his character, his integrity, and his mode of approaching work. I had met him while he was consulting at a company where I was employed. Assigned to work together on a project, we were just getting to know one another when his son, Adam, became critically ill. At one point, doctors figured that Adam had only a 40 percent chance of survival. Through all this anguish, my partner tried to balance his obligations with his overwhelming fear of losing his son. He always put Adam first, bowing out of all commitments to be at the hospital. I witnessed his devotion to Adam, and I was able to offer an ear and a strong shoulder as he talked of his fears and the horrible thought of life without his son. It was then that we became close as friends, and probably then that I knew that he shared my values and goals and that we could build a strong partnership. When it came time for us to launch a business, the blending of our minds and resources was first-rate. And the fact that we had become each other's best friend made it that much more pleasant.

Likewise, my current partner in WriteDirections.com and I had developed a professional association before we began working together. Beth and I were writers and entrepreneurs working solo from our home offices. We began to hold one another accountable for individual goals. Before long, we realized we shared the same goals, so we joined forces to offer coaching, consulting, and telephone and Internet classes in writing and marketing communications.

Unfortunately, the same positive outcome did not occur for Julia Starr, the friend I mentioned in Chapter 1, and her telemarketing firm. Julia, too, admired her partner, but her partner was also her lover. While business was good, both the professional and the personal relationships thrived. But when their business slowed down, due to Julia's desire to spend time with her child and a personal project, the partners began to argue about compensation and devotion to the company. Frustration quickly grew for both of them. If they had been just lovers, the relationship probably would have thrived—likewise if they had been just partners. Within five years, however, the combination proved to be the death of both relationships.

Had my friend Julia and her partner been married, the outcome might have been different, because their personal goals, especially financially, would have been shared goals. However, I also have seen many marriages either suffer or end because a husband and wife team eventually had no life together outside of work.

Through experience, my rule of thumb: business and social relationships go together like oil and water; they do not mix. Friendships, love relationships, and marriages are based on emotional ties—on the delicate and intuitive handling of personal feelings. In emotional relationships, you try to shield and support your loved ones from the obstacles and problems of daily life. The problem is that this sheltering instinct can have adverse effects on business relationships. To be successful, partners need to be able to have different opinions and the freedom to defend those opinions and to take actions without the concern of personally hurting someone else. If you're emotionally attached to your partner, it's almost impossible to defend those opinions and take those actions without hurting feelings.

For a friendship or any personal relationship to work, both parties must pledge their allegiance to one another; for a partnership to work, both parties must pledge devotion to the company, rather than to each other. Thus, the best partnerships are based on pure business.

However, compatibility is a big factor in forging a successful partnership. When my former partner and I first formed our company, a third partner was also involved. Although this third person had a heart of gold and was equally knowledgeable in our area of expertise, he didn't share the same goals for the company that we did. Hokey as it sounds, we wanted to build a successful company to make it possible for us to control our lives and to work together on projects we both enjoyed. Our third partner wanted our venture to remain part-time work, and he didn't want to have to deal with the administrative chores and financial investment that are involved in building a company. Eventually we bought him out, but not before tarnishing a friendship along the way.

As you contemplate a partnership, look for compatibility in the following areas:
- honesty
- approach to work
- personal and professional integrity
- money and financial matters
- fairness and treatment of others
- goals for the company
- attitudes about family and work priorities
- timeliness and punctuality
- honesty (it's worth mentioning twice)

If there's a negative history in any of these areas, you may want to reconsider taking on this person as your partner.

The best candidate will balance your strengths and weaknesses, cooperate on issues, work well with people, have good experience both in your field and in running a company, and be honest in every situation. You can start determining honesty by checking his or her background just as you would a potential employee's. Contact schools, former employers, and references and ask specific questions. If the potential partner has a history of conflicts with other people, you can assume it's just a matter of time before he or she betrays or turns on you, too.

Usually one partner needs to be "first among equals," at least for certain situations. One such successful partnership is that of Ann King and Ashley Ghegan, owners of the Blooming Cookies Catalog Company in Atlanta. Together they've built their company to $3.5 million in sales, growing at a rate of 30 to 35 percent a year and selling to 60,000 customers around the world. When I asked her to share advice for readers of this book, she offered this frank and wise counsel: "Having a partner can have its challenges no matter how well you think you know them. (Ashley's) responsibilities revolved around finance and operations. My role was more as visionary and new product development. For many years, we viewed the business in very different ways but also balanced each other. In the long run, however, the differences in how we view and feel about the company have become more pronounced. My experience has taught me that even in a partnership, one person has to be ultimately responsible for everything that happens in a business. If one person doesn't take responsibility, things fall through the cracks, or the decision-making process becomes too slow to remain competitive—paralysis by analysis. Perhaps the best analogy would be playing doubles in tennis. Both partners need to be strong, intuitive players and handle their side of the court. Whatever you do, though, some shots are going to go down the middle, and you have to know who will handle those shots. You can't say, 'You should have gotten it.' You have to know that one person, no matter what, is going to get it, and you have to know who that is from the beginning of the game."

Work with Virtual Partners

WHAT DO YOU DO IF YOUR IDEAL CANDIDATE FOR PARTNER lives on the other side of the country, or in a different country? Thanks to technology, you can form a well-oiled virtual partnership. My former partner and I had to operate this way for several years while I lived in Ohio and he lived in Maryland. The same rules apply as those in a traditional in-your-face partnership: you must have the same business and personal values. Honesty is more key than ever since you won't see one another at work very often, if at all.

87

Many of the clients I consult with have virtual partners, and I have worked with several people on virtual assignments—people I've never met face-to-face. Virtual arrangements of all kinds require the same basic attention to details: start with a signed agreement that includes everything from ownership division to confidentiality agreements, from non-compete contracts to compensation, from travel expenses to how phone bills will be handled.

Don't forget to take advantage of this arrangement when talking with outsiders. Imagine how impressed prospects will be when you mention that you have offices in two states.

Consider Outsourcing

ANY AREA THAT DOESN'T DIRECTLY CONTRIBUTE TO PRODUCING revenue, or any task you don't especially enjoy or for which you lack expertise, can be outsourced. The only way you'll get the time to do what you do best is to outsource some of the work.

Accounting, bookkeeping, graphic design, advertising, legal documentation, clerical work, and domestic work all can be outsourced. While I was running my firm, I hired a cleaning service and someone to mow my lawn. I know one professional speaker who, realizing that cooking dinner robbed her of her only available time with her two sons, hired a person to come into her home each night to cook dinner while she played with the boys. I also outsourced bookkeeping, graphic design (desktop publishing wasn't quite as simple then!), and some administrative work.

Any outside help leaves you with more time to spend with your company and the potential to be visible to your clients. Your options for outsourcing are many: from temp agencies to subcontractors to consultants to sales representatives to service organizations. Following are special considerations for dealing with some of these entities.

SUBCONTRACTORS AND CONSULTANTS

WHEN WORKING WITH SUBCONTRACTORS AND CONSULTANTS, always have a written agreement. Make sure the agreement includes a noncompete clause that protects you from their setting up their own shop and taking your clients with them.

As in any field, there are honest and dishonest consultants. I went into consulting because I have strong professional values and a very strong sense of independence. I considered myself a very honest consultant, even agreeing with my former partner early on that even though we could charge clients for a host of little expenses, we wouldn't do it. We decided we didn't want to nickel-and-dime the client. However, you should always practice caution when hiring consultants and subcontractors, because there's a reason that people like author Robert Townsend say, "Consultants are the people who borrow your watch to tell you what time it is and then walk off with it."

SALES REPRESENTATIVES

IN CHAPTER 1, I EXPLAINED THE TRAITS AND PERSONALITY OF an entrepreneur, noting that strong sales skills often are not among them. If you think this is true about yourself, outsource this important function to a sales representative so that you are free to focus on your business. Not only do sales reps help move your products, but they also suggest size and seriousness. Following are some ways to make the task a little easier:

◆ Understand that sales reps are independent contractors. Whereas a salesperson is someone who works for you and your company to sell your products, a sales representative is a free agent who represents your line of products or services but who works for other companies as well.

◆ Ask some loyal customers if they have any recommendations for sales reps. They may be able to provide names of good ones they've worked with. Other places to find names of good reps are through business owners in your field, at industry meetings and trade shows, and in the employment section of trade journals.

◆ Ask what other companies the representative works for. Make sure you're comfortable with the other products and services represented and that those goods do not interfere or take away from your product. Do not take on anyone who works for the competition.

◆ Select someone who needs a minimum of supervision and monitoring.

◆ Find someone who genuinely shares your excitement about your product or service.

◆ Check all references. Remember, your sales rep will be representing both you and your company to people and organizations that you may never have a chance to meet. Does this person do justice to the image you're trying to establish?

Look for an Angel

ANGELS HELP YOU COMPETE WITH BIGGER AND OLDER COM-panies by providing you with needed capital, all the while remaining silent, in most cases, which helps your company to be viewed as successful in and of itself. If you don't qualify for traditional bank financing, you might want to look for an angel. As the name suggests, an angel is someone who helps you; in this case, as a private investor. According to *Entrepreneur* magazine, the number of angel investors is impressive: more than 250,000 angels invest some $20 billion in the nation's businesses each year.

To find an angel, prepare a well-researched business plan, just as you would to seek traditional funding through a bank. Add an explanation of why someone should invest money in your business. Now begin networking in your field and seek out people who are successful and influential. Contact them in a professional way, just as you would were you seeking to sell your products or services. Offer to repay at a rate that is not insulting to your angel but is beneficial for you; or consider offering them stock if your company goes public. Give your angel frequent status reports or the opportunity to serve on your board of advisers.

HARNESS WELL-MEANING FAMILY AND EMPLOYEES

INVOLVING SIGNIFICANT OTHERS IN YOUR IMAGE-BUILDING CAMPAIGN

YOU MAY FIND YOURSELF STRAPPED FOR TIME AND RESOURCES as you attempt to cover all that's necessary to give your company that "big corporation" image. If you stay chained by the old "I'll do it all myself" habit, you will never move beyond the mom-and-pop level, which—although it keeps things comfortably informal and small—may leave you endlessly scratching along for a fair profit. If, however, you are willing to manage your business appropriately and daringly, you may be able to transform it into a competitive giant. If building a large company is your desire, then you had better start accepting the inevitable: others will have to share in the management of your business if it is to grow.

Rest assured that you can generally grow at your own rate. You don't have to have a staff of 200 people to look like a company of 200 people. Perhaps for now and as you grow, you only need help with administrative tasks or sales, and you've determined that you want someone on the inside *with a vested interest,* rather than an outside consultant, subcontractor, or partner. If this describes you, then you have at least two directions to consider.

Your Two Options

IF YOUR SMALL OR HOME-BASED BUSINESS IS SUFFERING from growing pains and you're convinced that you need help (this means you've read the first section of this chapter and don't want to continue going solo), then consider expanding. You have two options for developing a staff: family and employees. (Forget friends, because they won't be friends for long if they come to work for you.)

If you need help but want or need to save money, perhaps you should look no further than the person you share a cup of coffee with each morning. Bear in mind, however, that I have seen many a marriage go awry when spouses began working together. Things may come out equal when it comes to building a family, but it seems to work differently in business, as one person tends to take charge and the other must surrender authority. Besides, your way of operating may be what makes your business successful in the first place. If so, then you will want to find someone to assist you who is in tune with how you operate. A spouse may or may not fit that description.

If family does not seem to be the right option for expanding, then you may have to consider hiring help. However, I know firsthand that it's frightening to make the transition from self-employed to employer. There are so many negatives: additional accounting tasks (payroll, taxes, benefits, insurance) and, on the very personal side, bringing someone into your home or personal space (back rooms if at a business location) and sharing virtually every bit of knowledge about your business (and your home, if you work there). Initially, the thought of taking on all this employee-driven paperwork and loss of privacy seemed more intimidating to me than handling the workload by myself. If you feel this way too, then relax; other home-based and small business owners like me have done it successfully, and so can you.

There are other books available that outline intricate steps to take to expand your staff, so I'm going to discuss only those aspects of taking on staff that may affect your image. Your family and employees can be an image asset or a liability, depending upon how you train them to interact with your customers and talk about your company. This chapter addresses items to consider and to discuss with family in a conversational, nonthreatening, noninsulting manner. And, it provides a fifteen-item checklist that you can share with your family to ensure that they support the image you're trying to present.

Family

WHEN EMPLOYEES COME INTO YOUR HOME TO WORK OR invade the private back rooms of your small business location, they practically become members of your family—so it's easier if they're part of your family to begin with.

There are many advantages to pulling your family into the business:

◆ If slow times come, you can't let employees go without costly severance pay or other expenses; with family members, this is less of a concern.

◆ If you tap into help from your children, they will be exposed to a work environment and will come to understand better the logic of your working hours and routines at home.

◆ Being self-employed can be, quite literally, very taxing. With self-employment taxes reaching 15 percent and beyond, your net income can suffer. You can enjoy financial gains through tax savings by hiring your children. Since the government allows you to hire your children (under the age of eighteen) to do many miscellaneous tasks like filing, typing, and organizing, you can pay them a wage that may improve your bottom line by reducing your net profit and thus your tax bracket. That leaves you money to put back into the business to develop image-boosting materials! Remember: always check with your accountant first.

◆ You can talk about the intern in your office; no one needs to know he or she happens to be your own teenager.

On the flip side, there are disadvantages to pulling your family into the business:

◆ The line may begin to blur between work time and family time, making relationships suffer.

◆ Family members may expect compromise to carry into the work environment, whereas you, considering yourself the boss, expect your instructions to be carried out without discussion.

◆ Family members may not support your vision, your mode of operation, or your image-building techniques.

◆ Ownership begins to be assumed; the business suddenly no longer belongs to you but rather to the family, which means they feel free to call the shots.

If you don't want to hire family members or even have them help out in the office, discuss other ways that they can help. Here's what other home-based business owners have told me:

"Give your mom several of your promotional brochures to keep in her purse!" says Pat Merenko Smith, owner of Revelation Productions, which supplies biblical artwork around the world. "My mom is so proud of what I do that she always has several of my brochures with her to hand out. She tells everyone she thinks may be interested—and probably some who aren't—about my work. She actually told me that when she is in a parking lot and sees a car with a Christian symbol or bumper sticker on it, she will put a brochure in the window or under the windshield wiper! I have gotten many orders as a result of her unorthodox promotional methods.

And since my business is based on individual customer orders, it really does work."

Jay Massey of Coco Design Associates in Pensacola, Florida, says that emotional support is a gift his wife gives him: "All I can say is that my wife has to be the most understanding person alive. I am a work-at-home dad but not a housekeeper. On very busy or rainy days, our home and my office look like a madman and a four-year-old live there. Though she may be frustrated at times, she gives me a lot of understanding, knowing that I am staying home to benefit our child while trying to make something out of my business."

Of course, sometimes family can be an image liability too, as evidenced by Cindy Rojohn's experience. This speaker, trainer, and founder of CA Rojohn & Associates laughingly explains, "Since I work out of my home and provide a service, my dad assumes I don't work, even though he owned his own business. To this day, I can't figure out how he thinks I pay my bills, because when people ask him what I do, he says either I don't work or he doesn't know."

If your family is intent on helping but you don't want them working in your business, then explain to them how they can best provide support in other ways. See "Guidelines for Sanity and Happiness for Family Members of a Home-based Business Owner" on pages 96–97. After all, any stress or lack of support and understanding from your family will affect your productivity. Instead of arguing with them, find ways to include them in your business. You could discuss business situations with them (make sure you discuss more than problems) and ask their opinion or advice. Another option is to let them become a customer of your competitors! What better way to learn about your competition? Let your family learn about, observe, and gather all of the information you want. Have them do the following:

- pick up literature and marketing materials
- listen to a sales pitch
- observe customer relations
- investigate the size of the operation
- purchase and return an item
- contract a service

◆ talk to their employees about the competition (you)
In most cases, all family members will have to do is make a phone call requesting information or walk into their place of business and buy something.

Employees

AS YOUR BUSINESS GROWS, YOU WILL HAVE LESS TIME TO SPEND on administrative tasks. This means it's probably time to consider adding staff. Be forewarned, however: do not rush into hiring someone, because you may end up with the wrong person. In a small, expanding business, your customer contact means the difference between presenting a mediocre or an exceptional image, and possibly even between success and failure.

Take the time to hire right. Consider seeking the professional services of an executive recruiter, or for lower-level jobs, a well-respected employment agency. It may cost you a little money up front, but consider how valuable a well-suited person can be to the future of your business.

ITEMS TO CONSIDER

◆ **Know where you need help.** With which tasks do you need help? Administrative work? Sales? Marketing? Make a list of the responsibilities you want your employee to perform, and use it to form a job description. Although job descriptions aren't required by law, writing one has helped me focus on where I needed help, how much help I needed, and the type of person I was looking for to fill those needs.

◆ **Figure out what you can pay.** Remember that you're going to have as much as 30 percent in additional overhead above the salary you pay. This includes federal and state withholding taxes, Social Security and Medicare (FICA) taxes, long-term disability insurance, workers' compensation insurance, vacation and holiday pay, and other benefits. If you're like me, then your most intimidating thought about taking on an employee will be payroll and tax issues. After I realized that I would be taking on more work to have an employee, which defeated the purpose of getting an employee in the first

Guidelines for Sanity and Happiness for Family Members of a Home-based Business Owner

◆ Don't let children answer the business line—ever. And keep them out of the office when the phone rings.

◆ Ask if, when, and how your business owner would like the phone answered, then always accommodate.

◆ Shut the door if you don't want people (especially children) to hear the whoppers and frustrations that may be voiced from the home office.

◆ Never make assumptions or discuss details of the business or whereabouts of your business owner with a caller. Simply say that he or she is not available at the moment, instead of saying that he's taking the day off or out shopping at Staples. The less said the better. This way, the client can imagine your business owner is busy developing new products or servicing a client.

◆ Don't disturb the business owner's office; there may be perfect logic in why things are the way they are.

◆ Don't expect the business owner to be available for deliveries or to answer the home line. True, the person is right there at home, but such interruptions can destroy concentration and inhibit the freedom that one generally has in a typical office to come and go as needed.

◆ Just because your business owner may look to be on downtime, don't interrupt; even people in large offices have downtime yet still keep working. Remember, their downtime is business-thinking time, not relaxing "home" time.

◆ Understand that your business owner may get calls long after 5 P.M. and before 8 A.M. It's important to discuss together how afterhours business can still accommodate family life.

- Be supportive. Working from a home office can be frustrating and lonely.
- Arrange a signal—a gesture or message—with the business owner to designate when they're "at the office" and when they're "at home."
- Don't feel insulted if they seem to be ignoring you, especially if they don't check in with you every time they come and go. At those times, their mind is on work, not on family togetherness and responsibility.
- If you come home to a mess that your business owner made in the kitchen while hurriedly making lunch, just ignore it. Give a chance for it to be cleaned up after work. Then, if it's still undone, discuss it.
- Be prepared to watch more and more closet space disappear as boxes of products and office supplies multiply. Again, talk to your business owner to establish ground rules about how much of your home will be devoted to the business.
- Don't start talking until you can verify that your business owner is not on the phone. My home office was once situated so that people would start talking to me before they could see me. Many of my clients have heard my son eagerly and breathlessly running to me yelling, "Mommy, guess what?"
- Keep suggestions to yourself unless they're solicited. Pretend to be aware of only what your business owner tells you, since they're "at work" during the day. Thus, you know only what they "come home" and talk about.

place, I hired a part-time freelance bookkeeper instead. She took care of all of the administrative and bookkeeping duties I had originally thought an employee would do. I saved money and still got the job done. Problem solved.

◆ **Compare what you'll pay with what you'll get.** If you want to pay minimum wage yet expect some of the functions a CEO would perform, remember the old saying, "You get what you pay for." Sometimes reaching deep into the pockets to pay a little more will yield better results in the long run. And the better the employee, the better your image to clients.

◆ **Think through all aspects.** Before hiring someone, decide:
—Will I be able to tolerate this person for eight hours each day?
—Does he or she fit the image of my company?
—Will he or she support my customer relations and customer contact methods?
—If things don't work out, will I be able to fire this person without repercussions and hassles?
—Will I be able to discipline this person for inadequate performance without breaking their devotion to and enjoyment of the job?

◆ **Determine whether you can give employees what they want.** Make sure that you can (or are willing to) provide an employee with what he or she will need and want from a job. Here's a partial list:
—fair wages
—steady employment
—reasonable hours
—a comfortable work environment
—a sense that performance will be rewarded
—a feeling of being part of the team, of belonging
—an opportunity to contribute
—respect for the work, the management, the customers

◆ **Check references.** Insist references be provided (minimum of three), and check them all. Make sure finalists are who they say they are and have attended all the colleges or worked at the businesses they list.

◆ **Protect yourself.** Put new hires on a month-long probation. It's much easier for employees to be let go if they know going into the job that there will be a trial period.

◆ **Clean up your act.** If you practice some not-too-aboveboard techniques to build your company (such as some I've cautioned against in this book), the arrival of employees is a good occasion for evolving beyond those practices.

◆ **Be sure you're fully insured.** Get liability coverage in the event an employee is injured on your property.

KEEP 'EM MOTIVATED

MOTIVATED EMPLOYEES ARE A TRIPLE BLESSING FOR A BUSINESS; not only are they more productive and dependable, they also make excellent representatives. If you create a situation in which your employees can succeed and one in which they know their boss cares about them as individuals (not just as workers), then your employees will work harder.

If you can, tie employee pay to company performance. Employees should bear some of your company's risk. Even small businesses can set up a profit-sharing system in which employees earn a percentage of company profits for work well done. Profit-sharing is a minimal price for a business owner to pay for enhanced productivity and better customer relations. Provide details in writing to employees so that they understand there's a direct connection between the completion and quality of the assigned task and the reward. Your employees will quickly realize their level of income depends on the success of this business. They will report more on what the competition is doing, promote the business more during off-hours, and deliver better customer service than if they were paid just a straight wage with no hopes of any bonuses.

To carry out this incentive program, for example, tell non-sales employees that you will pay bonuses at the end of each year (or twice a year, for each six-month period—let employees vote on the frequency) in which the company increases sales and profits by 20 percent or more. Put sales representatives on commission and allow their earnings to be open-ended. If you don't put any limits on their earnings, then they won't put any limits on their selling.

If you opt against tying pay to performance, there are

other ways to keep employees motivated and performing at peak levels: seek their opinions, let them know that you value their ideas, and involve them in decision making.

Peggy Wight, president of Uncle Ralph's Cookies in Frederick, Maryland, says that she actively practices positive relations with her employees because "We took the time to hire right, and we value our employees, so we want to keep them. We also want them to be happy. We're like one big family here. We are very much a democracy."

So what does she do that works? "It's the little things that matter a lot," Peggy says. "I give them warm fuzzies for quality work. I also ask employees to tell me what I'm doing wrong with them."

While many business owners would think it unorthodox to ask employees how they want to be treated, Peggy takes it even one step further and asks employees what they want. "As a result we now have a book club that meets regularly, and we have one big birthday party each month for everyone who had a birthday that month. We also dress casually in the office each day, so for fun we now have one day a month in which we dress up in business attire.

"And when it comes to time off and holidays, we listened to what our employees wanted, too," Peggy says. "We used to give several paid vacation days off. Now, by employee consensus, we shut down between Christmas and New Year's and instead no longer pay for Fourth of July and Easter holidays. They get the whole Christmas week off with pay, and I feel especially good about that because they work so hard right before Christmas due to the incredible amount of Christmas orders we receive."

CUSTOMER SERVICE FROM EMPLOYEES

SUPERIOR CUSTOMER SERVICE CAN RESULT IN IMPRESSIVE SALES, because it is the best way to attract new business and to keep the old. Unfortunately, entrepreneurs can easily forget that they must retain the service factor regardless of how big and successful they become.

Years ago, long before Gateway Inc. was the giant it is today, I discovered them and purchased my first computer. I received excellent customer service and support. I bragged about my computer and recommended the company to all of my friends and clients. Years later, when it was time to move to a Pentium, I—without thought—turned immediately to Gateway again. This time I got a lemon. Not only did it not function properly, it—unknown to me until too late—tainted about twenty-five backup diskettes I had, which meant that original work was now destroyed. I had to spend weeks collaborating with my partner just to determine what information he had on his hard drive and spent the better part of three months, off and on, recreating documents. Meanwhile, I tried to get Gateway to take me seriously about the lemon I was sold. Even after I was able finally to get a regional service representative to come to my house (whereupon he discovered that my "new" computer had been built with a refurbished motherboard and sold as new), I still couldn't get the company to send me a new computer. Eventually, threats of using my journalism skills to bring this to the public's attention paid off, and they agreed to send me a replacement—provided I paid to ship the other one back, at a cost of about $95. After three more weeks of phone calls to them (during which I was put each time on hold for anywhere from six to forty-five minutes) and acrimonious discussions with supervisors and managers, I got Gateway to agree to pay for the return of the tainted computer. And what did I do? I switched to a Dell, got an excellent computer, and was back in operation within forty-eight hours of ordering it. I can't help but think that if Gateway president Ted Waitt had known personally about my situation, it would have been taken care of with no questions asked. Unfortunately, however, Gateway was on a growth spurt then, and for a while, their customer relations did not keep up with their sales. At the time, I was more or less an unknown without the contacts and reputation I have today, so getting through to Waitt personally at the time was not an option for me. I was, in short, a "regular" customer.

Today, Gateway is known for excellent customer service, and its computers are very highly rated. But for a time, the company lost sight of the direct relationship between success and customer service. Bottom line: The bigger the company becomes, the harder it must work to keep the service element strong. Awareness of this can be beneficial to you in two ways: (1) excellent customer service can help you stand out against the bigger companies, and (2) you will always maintain a reputation for top-notch customer service as you grow.

What else can you do to ensure quality customer service from your employees? Try these ideas:

♦ **Put guidelines in writing.** Create formal company standards and routines for dealing with customers, put them in writing, and make sure that each employee complies.

♦ **Assign ownership for customer complaints.** Make it a policy that whoever answers the phone owns the problem. Don't let a customer be passed around the office. Make it clear that whoever the customer talks to first is responsible for seeing that the situation is resolved. That employee doesn't have to be the one who actually resolves it, because of a lack of knowledge or authority, but immediate ownership can ensure that the problem is addressed in conjunction with someone who has the expertise or clout to do so. Top salespeople will tell you that "sales are the job of everyone in the business, not of a separate department."

♦ **Reward employees for customer service tips.** Require each employee to submit an idea at least once each quarter (or more frequently) for improving customer service. Build it into the job description and factor it into the annual evaluation as well.

♦ **Check up on employee interactions with customers.** Conduct periodic reviews of employee performance and production (and honesty) without prior notice. If you're not in the office all the time, change your routine and stop in unexpectedly. Call the company as if you are a potential customer. Have a friend or family member visit your business and make a purchase or discuss a service.

VIRTUAL EMPLOYEES

IF YOUR COMPANY IS LOCATED IN YOUR HOME OR A CRAMPED office, then you may be considering hiring a virtual employee. Like other aspects of employee relations, the pros and cons of hiring a virtual employee are best left to a book dedicated to human resources and employee protocols. What I'm concentrating on in this book is how a virtual employee can improve your ability to compete with the bigger, older, better-known companies.

One big advantage to hiring a virtual employee is that you can claim offices, or at least a representative, in another city, state, or even country.

A second advantage is that by eliminating the need for a large, formal office you may be able to offer your services to smaller businesses or products to consumers at lower, much more affordable prices.

A third benefit of hiring a virtual employee is that you can choose from a broader employee base. This best employee can be matched perfectly to your customer interaction needs.

TEMPORARY EMPLOYEES

SOMETIMES AN UNEXPECTED BIG ORDER COMES IN, OR YOU suddenly find yourself covered in stacks of paperwork. The natural reaction is to take on employees to handle the workload. It's important to stop at this point and think through the repercussions of acting too quickly: the order may be just a onetime occurrence, or perhaps your paperwork is unfinished because you took a week off to go on vacation. Thus, rather than hiring permanent employees, consider taking on temporary workers for short-term, infrequent, unpredictable, or seasonal situations. Besides avoiding the overhead that a search for permanent employees can bring, you won't be stuck with a hurriedly hired employee who doesn't fit the corporate culture. Also, employees require a lot of your time for discussions of their professional futures, the details of their benefits packages, their perceived need for more training and more challenges, and how their sick time and leave of absence options work. By using temporary employees you will have fewer interruptions and more time to continue your ongoing relationships with your clients, thus maintaining your appearance of size and success.

USE NETWORKING TO OPTIMUM ADVANTAGE

USING SAVVY OPPORTUNITIES
TO BUILD YOUR CONTACTS

NETWORKING IN ITS SIMPLEST FORM IS MAKING BUSINESS contacts and telling other people what you do. They may be customers, people who will give you leads for sales, contacts you find on the Internet, or people who can provide valuable information to improve your business or to give you a better understanding of the industry.

Is that marketing? Public relations? Cold-calling? Referrals? Recommendations? Building trust? Call it what you like, it all boils down to talking about what you do with the right people. Fortunately for small businesses, this is one area in which you can compete toe-to-toe with bigger, older, and richer companies, because networking is based on an inexpensive endeavor using a rudimentary skill: talking. And best of all, that talking is done between two people, regardless of the size of the companies behind them.

Years ago I held a dim view of networking. Its results weren't immediate enough for my "let's-make-it-happen-now" temperament, and I equated networking with standing uncomfortably at a conference with a cocktail glass in my hand, talking timidly about what I do for a living. Then a friend pointed out that *networking* is better than *not working* and that I should look at networking as accomplishing work and as the opportunity to replace cold calls with warm calls.

Through the years, as my experience in marketing and communication began to grow, I found myself lecturing clients to do more of it. I was telling clients that they needed to develop more contacts in their field and to exchange more information with prospects. I told students in my crisis communication seminars that they needed to meet the news media in advance and establish a relationship with them rather than waiting till a crisis hit to shake hands for the first time (Where's the trust at that point?). And I convinced a plastic surgeon that she should be more visible than her marketing director at her "Seminars of Optimum Beauty," because potential patients want to establish comfort and rapport with the person who's going to take a knife to their bodies, not with the person trained to deliver a marketing line. These are all examples of networking: being available, being visible, talking, reacting, responding, sharing, getting to know people, and letting them get to know you. These methods can lead to finding out who needs what and who offers what; what's happening in your industry, who's making it happen, and how; what concerns your prospects have; how others have solved the same problems you have; and how you can capitalize on your larger competitor's shortcomings.

Check the Numbers: Networking Has Power

WHAT CONVINCED ME OF THE VALUE OF NETWORKING WASN'T seeing it in action but rather realizing that quantitatively it has the potential to provoke action. My friend JoAnne decided she wanted to start selling health care products out of her home, but she had little start-up money to launch her business. Her question was how could she reach people without a large advertising budget? Besides writing a few informational news releases for her that were picked up by the local papers, I offered her some advice: get out and talk to everyone she knows. When she responded that this wouldn't get her very far because she didn't know many people, I challenged her to make a list of all the people she knows at least casually. Her list of 927 people astounded us both. Because she was involved in several civic organizations, I assumed that she would know more people than the average person, so I knocked about a third of the people off her list. I took the new number, 627, and decided that each of these people must know at least 627 other people. That meant that she could potentially reach more than 390,000 people if she talked to all the people she knew and got them to pass along information on her venture to the people they knew.

I still hate to network, but I do it because it's a tremendous way to build business, because the promotion goes on long after I have stopped talking. It takes a lot of "getting out there" and meeting and greeting and shaking hands and holding small—but purposeful—talk. I would still rather be delivering on services or managing my business, but I've learned that those things can't happen until I've done my share of networking.

I also credit my son's preschool with teaching me the value of networking. Each week, one child in Matthew's preschool class was allowed to bring an item for show-and-tell. The child would stand up in front of his peers and discuss the item. My son loves John Deere model farm machinery, so on one occasion he took in his favorite tractor. When I picked him up at day's end, one of the teachers mentioned that she had an old model barn that Matthew was welcome to since he loved tractors so much. Two days later, a mother stopped me in the hallway and said that her daughter, Matthew's classmate, told her that Matthew wanted a model corn picker but that John Deere didn't make them any more. The woman said she would sell me her corn picker for $10 since her son was older and had no interest in it anymore. One week later I got a call from another little boy's father, who said that he saw a picture Matthew drew of his toy tractor at school. He said he had extra tickets for a toy farm machinery show at the local fairgrounds and that since Matthew liked model farm machinery so well, we were welcome to have them!

As all parents know, play is a child's work. So all this happened because my son was brassy enough to talk about his "work" at school and advertise his love through a drawing. He obviously expressed himself well, convinced his audience of his love of farm machinery, and won them over so that they associated him with anything farm-oriented. Could there be any better lesson in the value of networking than that which works at an elementary level for a child?

How to Deliver the Most Impact

◆ **Know your prospects.** Determine how members of your target market get their information. What are their demographics and psychographics? What groups do they join? What publications do they read?

Peggy Isaacson, owner of the Florida-based human resources management firm Peggy Isaacson & Associates, says that she goes "where (my) competitors don't go. Many other human resources consultants join human resources business groups. Since that's not where my clients go, I join the groups my clients might join. My direct competitors don't usually do that—which often makes me the only one in the room who does what I do, which means that I'm the only human resources consultant my fellow organization members get to know. And who are they going to call if they need help or know someone who needs help? The bigger guys, just because they're bigger? No! They're going to call me."

As Peggy explains, "It's a comfort thing. Ninety percent of my business comes through networking, word of mouth, and referral. Networking pays better returns than advertising, cold-calling, or direct mail for me, because business owners and managers who are going to entrust their human resources needs to someone want to know that person or know someone who knows them."

◆ **Introduce yourself to everyone.** See "How Do You Describe Yourself?" in Chapter 1, pages 38–42. If you don't have time to deliver your whole introduction, prepare a clever one-liner:

—"I own a travel agency; I help people travel to their dreams."

—"I run an exterminating business; I help people rest soundly at night knowing that they and their pets are the only creatures in the house."

—"I'm a virtual assistant; I help my employers leap bothersome hurdles without having to move from their chairs."

◆ **Distribute your business cards generously.** Carry cards with you at all times. You never know where you'll make a contact. I've made contacts at the Y, at the local office supply store, through the driver of a towing service as he was pulling my car from an icy ditch, and at a wedding. (See Chapter 3 for more about distributing your business card creatively.)

Jay Massey of Coco Design Associates talks about the time an unusual networking opportunity worked for him: "I talk to just about anyone about just about anything. I find what they have to say interesting. Usually in American culture it will lead to that tacky question, 'So, what do you do?' I take that opportunity to introduce them to the concept of stay-at-home dads and answer, 'I stay home with my son and operate my graphics services business out of my house.' Then I drop a card. Very nonthreatening. One such dialogue with a small grocery store owner while picking up milk for my infant son led to my card being passed to the shop owner's brother, a man in the beginning stages of a new hotel franchise—a franchise in need of a logo. Lodging Hospitality Systems, the franchiser of Ashbury Suites and Inns, has been a client now for over three years. Just talking to people and caring about what they have to say is one of my best networking skills. Anybody can be a lead. Give them a card and go from there."

◆ **Get creative.** If you're at a gathering in which name tags are used, be the only organized one in the bunch: hang your business card from your name badge. It's a good conversation opener, and you will establish yourself as a little more creative than the other people present.

A couple of months after delivering a communication training seminar to NASA, I attended a conference hosted by the Chemical Manufacturers Association. My objective at the conference was to make contacts that might lead to more training. Below the name tag I was given, I pinned a copy of my business card that NASA had laminated for me with their insignia in small print on the right-hand side. Clearly the card was what I was advertising, whereas the NASA cover was merely what it was encased in. That little insignia, however, opened more conversations for me than I could have imagined. When asked about my association with NASA, I was able to tell listeners that I had conducted training sessions to help rocket scientists learn how to speak plain English to the public and the news media. Talk about a conversation starter! Luckily for me, the conversations happened to take place near the vendor booths of two of my larger competitors, so when listeners asked me to elaborate on my services, I smiled a sheepish smile, gestured toward the booths, and said, "I do what they do. . . only better." Of course, I laughed so that I wouldn't come across as arrogant. It worked. I was perceived as confident, capable, and in possession of a good sense of humor. Within a few months, I had phone calls from three contacts I made during those conversations.

◆ **Tell them what you want.** After you introduce yourself and tell them what you do, tell them what you are looking for and why you are there. Of course, you use diplomacy and tact in delivering your message. You don't say outright that you want new clients. But you do deliver the impression that you are very confident in what you do and that you are always receptive to new business. If you have a specific need, ask about it. If you don't ask, you won't get. In fact, if you don't ask, you won't even know if it's possible to get.

At the conference I just mentioned, I sometimes took a different approach in starting conversations with prospects. Rather than referring to my work with NASA, I summarized my experience and what my company provided, then asked advice on where I should continue to look to meet people just like the people I was talking to. I asked them to advise me on the types of training these referrals would be looking for and why they would or would not hire an individual like me and my company. Not only did I receive great feedback because I was making these people feel important and knowledgeable, but I was asked by several of them to forward my company information. Within a year, I had two large long-term contracts as a result of that conference.

◆ **Keep your foot out of your mouth.** Always stay focused on who you are talking to and what you want to accomplish as you network. Even though your target may be free-spending, freethinking teenagers, for example, you don't want to act like one to a senior citizen with whom you are trying to network for information or contacts. Instead of seeing you as suitable for the market you're trying to reach, they'll assume you aren't professional enough to make it in business.

During my interviews for this book, I came across dozens of entrepreneurs willing to share their most embarrassing experiences of foot-in-mouth disease; however, I reserved this opportunity to tell one of my own. Years ago while teaching a class for the Risk and Insurance Management Society on crisis management—a class made up of professionals from around the world in various industries— I established a rapport with an executive from UPS. I networked with him (as opposed to "marketed" him) about my company's services, what we were looking for, and how we could reach more individuals like him at other companies. While drawing the conversation to a close after the class so that we could each dash for a taxi, he asked me to send him information on one aspect of my services. I, in my haste to get to the airport, replied, "Sure, I'll Fed Ex that to you as soon as I get back."

◆ **Be discreet; respect confidences.** When I was a journalist, I learned quickly that if you want sources to open up a second time, then you'd better respect their request for "off the record" the first time. In business, the words "off the record" aren't mentioned as much as they are assumed to be understood. Therefore, you have to be savvy enough to understand confidences between two parties. Just because Person A puts you in touch with Person B doesn't mean that you can suggest to Person B that you and Person A are good friends or that he or she is a satisfied client. Make sure you ask Person A whether or not you can share a referral, a story, a good experience, an endorsement. You will notice in this book that at times I mention a client's name and at other times I don't. Although all my examples are based on experience, I have respected the wishes of those clients who prefer to remain anonymous. It's good business.

◆ **Maintain contacts over time.** Even as the focus or intent of your work or your company changes, keep networking with people you know.

Peggy Isaacson says this worked well for her: "Several

years ago I talked with a fellow I knew at my last corporate job. I'd been laid off a year before he was. He landed a great position in a hospital near my home, so he gave me a tour and told me about his new job. Some time later he called with a referral that resulted in a training relationship with a client for several years. Years later, I had a conversation with the CEO of that same organization; he was now with another company and wanted to know if I would work with his new organization. This resulted in a yearlong contract. So staying in touch with one former colleague resulted in long-term relationships with two new clients."

◆ **Explain your uniqueness.** Make sure the people you network with know what sets you apart from your competition. (See Chapter 4 for more about finding your unique selling point.)

A business I consulted with near Chicago delivered gift and gag items using employees who dressed in costumes and delivered a song or speech or whatever unusual form of presentation a client would request. Their marketing problem was that they had a hard time explaining to the public the wide scope of their offerings and their ability to service the customer in unique and individualized ways. I suggested that the owners develop a series of two-minute humorous or heart-warming stories about deliveries they had made and begin recounting those at local functions and other speaking engagements. The stories were hits and business picked up quickly, especially after a local disc jockey heard one and asked them to share it on his talk show. That led to his calling the business occasionally so that listeners could hear the latest embarrassing or heart-wrenching tale. Of course, this exposure built public awareness of the business and gave prospects ideas on how to use the company to send messages to their friends. It also positioned the company as unique in its services and as being a fun-to-deal-with and customer-pleasing organization. Its credibility improved tenfold.

If you are in a well-established and well-understood field such as plumbing or retail gifts or children's clothing, you won't feel concerned about communicating the basics of

Where to Find Networking Opportunities

THE PURPOSE OF NETWORKING is to connect one-to-one with as many people as possible so that you know them and what they can do for you, and so that they know you and what you can do for them. Opportunities for networking are everywhere. Here are some of the places I've had it work for me or seen it work for others:

◆ professional groups
◆ networking groups
◆ breakfast clubs
◆ standing in line
◆ parties
◆ political debates
◆ public speaking situations
◆ schools
◆ colleges
◆ community service meetings and events
◆ hotels
◆ airports
◆ airplanes
◆ subway rides (everyone's nose isn't buried in a book)
◆ charitable functions
◆ children's birthday parties
◆ churches and synagogues
◆ bars
◆ restaurants

what you do. This can be a mistake. Whereas an unusual business like a specialty delivery service may have to elaborate on its offerings just so that people can understand the nature of what it offers, a well-established business is rather self-explanatory, so owners forget that they need to elaborate on what makes them unique.

◆ **Network in every situation.** Don't take for granted the comfort and downtime you spend talking with friends and

- volunteer service situations
- Toastmasters
- health clubs and gyms
- professional associations
- chamber of commerce meetings
- neighbors' and friends' homes
- casual conversations with colleagues
- weddings
- funerals
- amusements parks
- during intermission between performances at the Kennedy Center (replace with a theater local to you)
- social circles, such as community picnics and block parties
- conversations with former customers, clients, or patients
- stores (Home Depot, Staples, Bloomingdale's, to name a few in my experience)
- coffee shops
- bus trips
- ferryboat rides. (Thanks, by the way, to Jim from Los Angeles, who not only loaned me his cellular phone to make a call as we rode the ferry from Ellis Island back to New York City but also directed me to a prospect who hired me for some consulting work. And thanks to Jim also for helping me prove that you never know when someone you meet can help you on your quest.)

relatives. Be a serious and committed person of integrity with everyone; you never know when it might come back to bless you, as it did for Ralph and Peggy Wight, owners of Uncle Ralph's Cookies in Frederick, Maryland.

The Wights struggled with their business for the first few years, until a friend from Michigan loaned them some seed money that allowed the company to take off. "He approached us. It was a big step for us at the time, but he saw our potential," says Ralph. As Peggy explains it, "We had lived in Michigan for several years before moving to Frederick seventeen years ago. We made a friend out of another mom-to-be and her husband in one of my childbirth classes. As it turned out, the family was rather wealthy, and it was their father who decided to invest in us." That networking paid off: sales for Uncle Ralph's Cookies last year were posted at just under $4 million.

◆ **Join a networking group.** Perhaps the most well-known networking group is Business Network International (BNI). You can call 800-825-8286 or check out www.bni.com for a BNI group near you. Each member enjoys profession exclusivity; in other words, each group has only one contractor, one financial planner, one graphic designer, one publisher, and so on. Meetings involve giving brief presentations about your work and letting the audience know what types of referrals would be helpful.

◆ **Offer referral rewards.** Tell existing clients and other contacts that you reward referrals that lead to new business. You can reward them with dinner at a local restaurant, a gift, a gift certificate, or a discount on their next invoice. At my former company, I offered anyone who provided me with a lead that led to a contract at least 5 percent of the net profits of that contract. In instances where clients felt a conflict of interest in accepting such a reward, Santa would send them an appreciation gift at Christmastime, or I simply took them out for dinner at the nicest restaurant in town.

Turning Daily Routines into Opportunities

MASTER THE TELEPHONE

ADDING CREDIBILITY EACH TIME THE PHONE RINGS

HETHER INVOLVED IN BUSINESS OR pleasure, we have become a society of phone-toting paranoiacs concerned with "staying in touch." I've seen people carrying cell phones at the beach, at water parks, at the theater, and at Disney World. No one wants to miss a call. For entrepreneurs, however, just getting the call is not enough; we have to be equally concerned about "working" the call. Depending upon the nature of your business, your only contact with many clients may occur over the phone, making your telephone presence your number-one image builder.

Since you don't get a second chance to make a

good first impression, look upon your telephone as your front door. The words that greet a caller, the background noise, and even the number of times the phone rings will give callers impressions about your business. Companies have become so aware of the importance of effective telephone communication that SkillPath Seminars—just one of dozens of seminar companies—has taught 80,000 people in the past five years how to use the phone appropriately. Copresident Denise Dudley reports that "teaching just customer service and telephone skills is a $2 million business for us."

Unfortunately, too many entrepreneurs think they're pretty good at using a telephone; after all, they've been doing it for years. However, cold-calling is so important to the success of a small business that just being good isn't enough. If you're owner, president, and director of marketing, everything you dislike about using the telephone is magnified, because you may be the one handling all the calls. To master the telephone, you'll have to tackle the depersonalization of phone communications and be as effective on the phone as you would be face-to-face.

Your Equipment

WHEN IT COMES TO TELEPHONES, ASSOCIATED EQUIPMENT, and services, it's time to splurge. Buy or lease the best (and generally most expensive) system or service you can justify. As a lone worker (or one of just a few) you will probably keep irregular office hours, because you will be out tending to deliveries, making contacts, or dropping calling cards. When those efforts start paying off in phone calls, each call could be vitally important to you. It is essential that every call be answered promptly and professionally.

Regardless of the location of your business, its size, or its products or services, you can do business with almost anybody from virtually anywhere, thanks to the telecommunications boom of the past ten years. With state-of-the-art telephone equipment and services available these days, you can give the appearance of operating a major corporation, even though the truth may be that you're anything but. However, before laying out a lot of money for that equipment, recognize and accept that what you are paying for today may be outdated tomorrow—that's how fast telephone services, equipment, and voice messaging options are changing. Whatever your telephone service of choice, be sure that it is a service or piece of equipment that can easily handle—or be updated to accept—the options that will be available tomorrow. I recommend dispensing with phone answering machines and looking into answering services or voice messaging options. Interactive voice messaging provides you with combined mobility and immediate contact with clients. Plus, only you will be able to access calls (has your family ever played back a message on your answering machine and accidentally deleted it?). You won't have to worry about losing messages (has your electricity ever gone out, rendering your answering machine useless?), and your professional presence will be greatly enhanced by the options a voice messaging service provides (why do so many answering machines have those irritating beeps anyway?).

Recognizing that voice messaging may not be for you or your budget, I have provided tips on answering machines and answering services throughout this section. Remember that telephone service options are increasing every day, so you would be wise to contact service providers in your area to learn what your options are. For example, at the printing of this book it's hard to imagine voice messaging getting much better (although I know it will), because the options are already reasonably priced, readily accessible, and sophisticated enough to make any home-based operation sound like a corporate behemoth. With what is currently available on the market, you can have one service that will:

◆ locate you at any number of your choice in the world
◆ treat your callers to up-to-the-minute news headlines from CNN News Radio while they wait
◆ allow a caller to choose from several options, including leaving a message for the general office or your personal mailbox or sending a fax
◆ let you then retrieve that fax at any fax machine in the world
◆ allow you to set up conference calls with several people, all by pressing just one key and then the various individuals' phone numbers
◆ read your computer e-mail messages to you over the phone and allow you to reply to each message with the press of a key
◆ provide you with options supporting the suggestion that you are a solid, sizable company. For example, let's say you are a one-person organization. You can purchase voice messaging for one business line and have the receiving message answer thus: "Hello. You have reached XYZ International. All lines are busy right now. If you would like to leave a message for the general office, press 1. If you know the party with whom you wish to speak, press the first letter of that person's last name now." Now, let's say that your name is John Smith. After that person presses 7 for S on his phone

keypad, he will hear: "To speak with David Powell, press 1; to speak with Michelle Rice, press 2; to speak with John Smith, press 3." All the messages, regardless of whom the caller attempts to reach, go into one voice mailbox, which you can retrieve from anywhere at any time by dialing one number. You can actually program in up to two dozen names.

In short, telephone messaging options today are limited more by your imagination than by your budget.

Preparing Your Equipment for Calls

◆ **Get a business line.** Sure, residential lines are less expensive per month and offer cheaper calling rates, but your company will not be listed in the telephone directory as a business. You might lose business if potential clients are not able to find your company in the phone book. Being accessible and easy to find are important even if your business is not dependent on a local clientele. When you give talks and advertise in publications nationally, for instance, publishers and sponsors tend to list only your company name, city, and state, but no phone number. I have had several clients tell me that they had seen an article I had published and, because my company's name and address were included at the end, they were able to locate me through a telephone directory or directory assistance.

◆ **Get two more lines, for your fax and Internet connections.** With one line, you might frustrate your callers with a busy signal or an endless loop into voice mail purgatory. Think about the callers' perceptions when they get a busy signal. They wonder: "Can't this company afford enough lines? Are they understaffed? Are their employees out of the office all the time? Don't they think my business is important?"

◆ **Register as a business with the phone company.** Doing so generally gets you a free listing in the yellow pages under the category of your choice, but choose this category carefully: under what subject area would your clients *most likely* try to find you? If in doubt, ask two or three trusted clients where they would look to find you. Their answers may surprise you.

◆ **Keep your phone lines separate.** That is, keep your home telephone extensions away from your office area. You don't want a client to hear background noise such as a home line ringing endlessly or, worse yet, home-oriented chatter from a family member.

◆ **Be careful with answering machines.** If you insist on using one, then at least make sure it's not the kind that cuts off after a few seconds. Replace it with one that will let callers talk as long as they want.

◆ **Make sure your telephone has a hold feature.** Learn how to use it! When running a business from home, for example, you never know when unexpected noises, doorbells, beeps, and barks will sound.

◆ **Use hold time wisely.** While a customer is on hold, provide him with more than dead air. How? With a messages-on-hold system, you can provide your caller with local radio music, the news, your office hours, or better still, a pre-recorded message about your company and your services. It's probably worth it if you put ten or more callers on hold each day. At the end of one week, that would mean you've marketed to at least fifty potential customers. Caution: These messages can get annoying if they're short and on a repeating loop, or if the customer is placed on hold a lot.

Also consider making that wait worth your customers' while. In your on-hold message, provide a word or phrase they can use to get a discount or unexpected bonus. Be creative. Just be sure to change the special word or phrase at least once per week. If you're looking for the opportunity to introduce a new service, then offer customers on hold a question they should ask when you return to the phone, and let them know that for listening to the answer, they'll receive a discount. The impression? What a clever company you have!

◆ **Avoid call-waiting.** Generally call-waiting lives up to (or down to) its other distinction as call-*hating*, because invariably someone has to be placed on hold. The impression this creates is that you are either small or not very well staffed. Find out what options your phone company and local voice messaging services can offer. Also, several inexpensive prod-

123

ucts are now available that support several phone and data lines and offer important business features like call forwarding to an answering service while you're on the line—a positive alternative to call-waiting. Some of these products work alone, others in conjunction with your PC.

If you just can't afford the extra pennies for voice mail, then consider getting call-waiting on your standard business line. A busy signal does more than tell the caller that no one is available; it indicates that the person they're calling is affiliated with a very small business. With call-waiting, you can put people temporarily on hold while you are answering the other line. However, putting someone on hold to take another call can anger the party you're talking to and can make you look understaffed. Here are two techniques to try: (1) Tell the first caller that you have another call coming in and have to take it because you have been waiting for it all day, but that it will take only about fifteen seconds to handle. Then find out who caller number two is, promise to call him back, and return to caller number one as quickly as possible. Don't do this more than once, however; the implication is that the other caller is more important than the one you were talking to first. And don't do this at all if you are the one who initiated the call. After all, if you were expecting an important call, why would you tie up your line by calling another client, or why didn't you tell the client when you first started talking that you might have to interrupt the call? (2) Be frank about the second call; say, "May I put you on hold for about twenty seconds while I get the other call? I'm the only one here right now."

◆ **Avoid cordless phones.** At least, don't have a cordless phone as your primary office phone. Cordless phones require electricity. Thus, if the electricity goes off, clients have no way of reaching you.

◆ **Set up an 800 number.** If you plan to take many orders over the phone, or if your customers are long-distance, then get an 800 number. Note, however, that this can be costly. Then again, if you are selling a product nationally, can you afford not to have an 800 number?

◆ **Get a clever phone number.** Negotiate with the phone company for a number that has a word relevant to your business in it. For example, management planning consultants may want to pursue 555-PLAN (7526), or a pesticide business may want to offer customers 555-BUGS (2847). If the number is unused, it generally doesn't cost anything to secure it.

◆ **Be cautious with fax transmissions.** Although a fax uses a phone line, remember that it is just like mail but without the envelope. Don't send anything confidential through a fax machine. Also, double-check the phone number; after all, we often misdial when calling to talk to someone—the same could happen when faxing. Imagine faxing a quote to Client A that was meant for Client B, especially if you already provided a quote to Client A that was higher in price for the same service or product.

◆ **Review your communications system at least once a year.** Telecommunication technology advances at a rapid rate, and phone service providers are regularly adding features that you might use. With the growth in the number of home-based businesses, most phone companies have created special departments to serve the needs of entrepreneurs.

Preparing Yourself for Calls

◆ **Keep a small hand mirror nearby.** Use it when you're talking on the phone. Corny, you say? Perhaps, but studies show that when we are smiling, our voices sound more positive and energetic. Use the hand mirror to note when you need to smile.

◆ **Sit up straight.** When you're on the phone, you want your voice to sound its best; to do that, you need good posture to open your diaphragm.

◆ **Stand up.** Even better than sitting up straight is standing up. You sound more energetic and distinct when your entire body is vertical because your diaphragm is open. My former partner and I learned this by accident. During one of his routine daily calls to check in with me, I commented that he sounded particularly dynamic and positive. He noted that the only difference from the other phone calls was that he was standing up. Out of curiosity, we experimented with the technique during subsequent calls. I guessed correctly each time he was standing.

◆ **Tape-record your side of your conversations.** Listen to them occasionally. Your verbal impression is very important to instilling confidence in the caller, especially if you're talking with a potential client for the first time. Listen to the speed, tone, and inflection of your voice, the eloquence of your words, and the overall presentation and personality that you impart. Would you be impressed with this delivery?

◆ **Plan your calls in advance.** Know what you are going to say. Take the time to write or type out your thoughts. This avoids the embarrassing situation of having to call people back with afterthoughts and questions.

◆ **Announce who is calling immediately.** If you don't and the person you're calling doesn't recognize your voice, you've put the customer in an awkward position.

◆ **Don't eat or chew gum.** And don't do anything in the background that makes noise. You want the person you're calling to think they have your undivided attention. Likewise, don't type, open mail, or read e-mail when you're on the phone. Callers can tell if you're distracted.

◆ **Take notes on what the other person says.** They can't see you writing, so why not rely on a short note rather than an unreliable long memory?

◆ **Have tidbits ready.** Jot notes in advance of impressive bits of news or statistics on your industry's trends and accomplishments. Then, when a potential client is on the phone, take the opportunity to work those statistics into your conversation. Your client doesn't know that you're referencing crib notes or index cards, or even notes you've taped to the ceiling (it's your office, after all).

◆ **Keep a motivational phone message by your phone.** Remember what I said about looking upon your telephone as your front door, since it may be the only route into your company. I once conducted an executive crisis management training program for UPS. Upon arriving at its world headquarters in Atlanta, I was greeted by a security officer. He was gracious, professional, and very visitor-oriented. I noted that on the back of his workstation was his reminder for his role: a plaque that read "Director of First Impressions." It may be a good idea to write that same message on an index card and tape it by your phone.

Receiving Calls

◆ **Don't answer on the first ring.** The appearance will be that you have nothing better to do than wait for the phone to ring. You didn't pounce on every incoming call in your old office, so why do it now? Give yourself time to psychologically detach from your home or the work you were doing. Likewise, don't wait until the fourth ring; callers will immediately begin to imagine reasons why it takes your company so long to answer, such as customer service is a low priority at your establishment.

◆ **Keep children and pets away.** Teach your children not to answer your business phone and not to make any noise while you are on the phone. Likewise, keep pets, especially dogs and birds, away from phones when you're talking to someone. One bark or tweet and the gig is up!

◆ **Enlighten your family.** Explain to your spouse how you want the phone answered and messages handled. Post a note over the phone with the words you want said; for example, "Hello. You have reached XYZ International. How may I direct your call?"

◆ **Be confident.** Answer the phone with an overpowering confidence. Instead of "Hello," make it "Good MORNING! This is JOHN SMITH. How may I HELP YOU?" Think of how you feel when someone answers with a weak hello and mumbles. Be confident! It's infectious!

◆ **Be accessible for calls.** If you must be out of the office regularly, be sure your customers can get in touch with you when they need to. Use a voice messaging system, and consider a cellular phone and pager. Or check with your local telephone service provider about the availability of a one-number service, which is a single telephone number that can be programmed to find you when you're not in your office.

◆ **Establish a "best time" to call.** If your business is such that clients may have to call you periodically, then provide them a best time to call. Structure your day so that clients know they can reach you (for example, plan to work in your office between eight and ten every morning and do on-the-road activities after ten). It can be irritating for clients to get an answering service or voice mail and have to wait for a call-back. If it happens frequently, the fact that no one else is in your office to answer the phone will be that much more apparent. Besides, sales are rarely made between a machine and a customer.

◆ **Ignore dead air.** Don't fall victim to silence by filling it with every thought you have. Give yourself time to think before you talk. The impersonal nature of the telephone tends to make users feel compelled to keep talking since they can't see the person they're talking to.

◆ **Learn to use your mute button.** One way to keep from inserting your foot in your mouth is to use your mute button. While I was writing this chapter, I decided to polish my skills at using the Microsoft Excel program to better organize my consulting and coaching work. I called a couple of local training companies for prices and dates. At the second company, a man answered the phone and listened attentively to my request. But then, rather than responding "One moment, please," and placing me on hold, he shared his every thought with me, saying, "I'm not sure if we have anybody here who knows that program well enough to teach it or not; hold on a second. . . hey, Bob, you know Excel well enough to teach it?" I couldn't hear Bob's reply. A few seconds later, the man came back on and said, "Yes, Ma'am, we can do that for you. Would you like to set up a time?" My response: "No thank you." My thinking? "Not in a million years."

◆ **Record someone else's voice.** Have someone else put the voice message on your answering machine or messaging service. An unfamiliar voice implies yet another person in the organization. Scout around among friends and neighbors for the person with the perfect phone voice.

◆ **Create a polished voice-mail message.** Depending upon your unique circumstances, you may not want to use an answering service or elaborate voice-mail service. If, for example, you are a consultant and it's not as important for your customers to perceive your company as big as it is for them to know when you are available, then create a professional voice-mail message and change it daily. Write a script to use when you record your announcement so that you don't inject "uhs" or forget pertinent information. Tell them how to skip your announcement to immediately leave their message. Then identify your company, yourself, and the day and date, and indicate your availability (will you be out of the office that day? in tomorrow?). Also include when callers can expect to hear from you.

◆ **Keep it short.** The best phone answering messages are short ones; however, it is OK to add a tag line about the company. Examples: "You have reached XYZ International, the first company to provide widgets from coast to coast," or "Thank you for calling XYZ International, widget providers to ten *Fortune* 500 companies."

◆ **Deliver on promises.** In your message, state that "One of us will get back to you as soon as possible." Or, better still, say that "One of us will get back to you (when)," then give an exact time frame: before five o'clock, within four hours, by tomorrow. Be sure you stick to the promise.

◆ **Encourage others to answer the telephone.** If you work at home, have your spouse (or significant other) answer the phone (in a professional manner, of course) before passing the call on to you. The impression? That you have a receptionist or secretary.

◆ **Solicit feedback.** After someone calls to place an order, follow up through the mail with a standard form designed to solicit feedback on the telephone etiquette of the person who handled the call. Big companies continually solicit feedback on how they're doing.

◆ **Convert e-mail to voice mail.** The business world is becoming accustomed to sending messages via e-mail and expecting timely receipt of those messages. Unfortunately, this further exhausts home-based business owners, who already find it hard enough to be everywhere they should be. The answer? Subscribe to a service that allows you to hear e-mail messages over the telephone using text-to-speech technology. Thus, while you're away from the office, you can convert e-mail to voice mail so that you can get your messages while they're still timely. The impression is that you or your office is reliable, organized, and available enough to retrieve messages quickly.

Making Calls

- ◆ **Sound upbeat.** Always sound friendly, energetic, positive, and upbeat. If potential clients indicate that they have time to talk, then don't worry that you are interrupting them to talk about your product. Because you believe in what you offer, you know that you are offering a solution—in the form of a product, service, or information—to someone who needs your help. (However, always be aware and respectful of a client's time and schedules and the fact that they weren't expecting your call.)
- ◆ **Be respectful of the people you're calling.** Don't try to hasten a relationship or create artificial feelings of goodwill by using first names with people you are cold-calling. Sounding too familiar and relaxed with strangers will immediately make them uncomfortable. Think how you feel when a telemarketer calls and immediately addresses you by your first name!
- ◆ **Be prepared.** When calling a client, always be ready to leave a message. Sometimes the person you want to speak to will not be there. Prepare in advance a script of what you want to say, or write down bullet items so you won't ramble or forget anything and have to call back.
- ◆ **Don't be cute.** Don't leave comical or sarcastic messages on voice mail. Unlike in a face-to-face conversation, you can't be there to explain if the message fails in its intent.
- ◆ **Try it again.** If the answering system where you're calling provides the option of erasing the message and trying again, then be sure to listen to the message that you leave. If you do not like what you said or how you said it, do it again.

◆ **Watch background noise.** Don't leave messages from noisy restaurants or bars. The background noise will make more of a lasting impression on your client than the details of your message.

◆ **Add the right noise.** Consider purchasing an audiotape that features the sounds of a busy office in the background, if you want to add that impression on the phone.

◆ **Watch your timing.** Be conscious of the time when leaving a message on voice mail. Generally, it will be stamped with a time at the receiving end. Ask yourself, if you worked outside of your home and/or for a very large employer, would you be calling at 10 P.M.?

◆ **Keep the opportunity available.** Do not leave your phone number when the potential client you are calling has not yet met you and has no idea why you called. If you do, you will probably never receive a return call, and that puts you at an awkward disadvantage when you have to call again. Simply say, "This is John Smith with XYZ International. I'm calling about (leave a brief message). I will try to reach you again tomorrow." Sound positive and upbeat.

◆ **Be courteous to everyone.** Always be polite, especially with every secretary or personal assistant you talk to. At your old job, you may have brushed off most of these people when calling customers, but not anymore. Just as when you're making a sales call in person, these people can stand between you and your contact by phone, too. Slight a secretary who has his or her boss's ear, and you may never gain access to that boss again. In fact, when you make a preliminary call to the company's general number before calling on a new prospect, get the full name of the secretary, too. Give that name as much respect as your contact's name.

◆ **Forget gimmicks.** Unlike what some salespeople would have you believe, there are no magic words to guarantee a sale over the phone. Honesty and an organized delivery with purposeful, directed messages, combined with a listening ear, make the most sales. Management author Peter Drucker has said that "the most important thing in communication is to hear what isn't being said."

The Fine Line Between
Deception and Impression

BY FAR, THE LONGEST LIST OF QUESTIONABLE PRACTICES
other entrepreneurs have shared with me falls under the category of telephone techniques. I consider the following my
top four candidates for dubious distinction only because
three or more individuals have shared each of these techniques with me and swear by the results.

1 Calling back to your office "for messages" from a client's
office (within earshot, of course) and having a phone "conversation" in front of your client. Even if you're just talking
to your answering machine or voice mail, you can have
some rather impressive one-sided discussions about another successful contract or a very satisfied customer. One
engineering consultant said he used this technique once to
"converse" about toxic release projection reports, a service
he hadn't yet marketed to his current client because he
didn't want to give the impression that he was hungry for
work. As he had hoped, the client did eavesdrop on the
conversation, then asked him about the service. He walked
out with a new assignment.

2 When a client calls, saying, "I'm in the conference room;
could you hold while I transfer this to my office?" The idea
is to put the person on hold, then walk around your office
once so that your voice will sound different when you return
to the line. While you're walking, you mentally turn your sur-
roundings from a conference room into your office. After all,
your office is your conference room, too, right? And your
boardroom and your training room.

3 During phone conversations, blaming any minor disorganization or loss of memory on an outside source that by its
mere mention makes you sound larger: "My office is cleaned
every Wednesday (or whenever), so things get moved
around. Could you hold a moment while I find that file?"
(Of course, you don't mention that you are the one who does
the cleaning.) You would use that moment to regain your
composure or to get organized before returning to the call.

4 If customers come to you, creating a dog and pony show. One man I know started a computer software training company in the business district of a large city. His location meant that he received a considerable number of inquiries from people stopping by during lunch breaks. Because he was equipped to expand long before he had the clients to merit growth, his large office featured many empty desks. To make a positive impression on the people who stopped by, he placed photographs, personal belongings, and paperwork on the empty desks. Then he instructed the employees he did have to take turns dialing the receptionist each time someone walked through the door.

As with the other questionable ideas I share in this book, I do not condone these; I want to acknowledge that they exist and counsel against them. Honesty, as I've said, is still the most redeeming and successful business practice you can adopt.

A Routine Call Turns Sour

WHAT SHOULD HAVE BEEN A ROUTINE CALL TO A CLIENT turned into a detriment to management consultant Michael Field's reputation. His mistake? Michael didn't remember the telephone feature of dialing *67 before a phone call in which he didn't want the recipient of the call to note (and be able to call back) the phone number from which he was calling. He explains:

"Because I work at home, I sometimes take advantage of the freedom it provides me in completing errands when the rest of the world is at their nine-to-five job. I never wait in line at the bank on Saturday mornings, and I don't have to call the dentist five months in advance to secure an evening appointment. Likewise, I get my car serviced during the week at Jiffy Lube, when the line is always short. One day when I took my car in for an oil change, I took along a report a client asked me to review. I knew that all he wanted was good feedback; he didn't need to know where it was done, at a corporate office complex, in my comfortable home office, or in the waiting room at Jiffy

Lube. While I was reading, I discovered I needed clarification on an item. Rather than pay the expensive rates from a cellular phone, I asked the owner of the Jiffy Lube if I could use his quiet office to dial the client's 800 number. After getting the information I needed, I returned to work. However, the next call that came in to Jiffy Lube was for me. It was my client hoping to add more information that he had forgotten to share during the first phone call. Unfortunately, the phone wasn't handed to me until it had already been answered, 'Hello. Thank you for calling Jiffy Lube where no appointments are necessary. How may I help you?' After recovering from my embarrassment and explaining the situation to my client, I learned that he had gotten the number from his receptionist's phone, which records the numbers of all incoming calls. From that moment on, every time I received work from that client, he would ask— half jokingly—if I was going to give the work serious consideration or if I planned to take it along while doing errands."

What would Michael do differently? In addition to dialing *67 before each call, he says he would be sure to give his cell phone number and tell the client to call him at that number with any further thoughts.

Can an Answering Service Contribute to Your Image?

TO ANSWER THIS QUESTION, I TURNED TO VOICE RESPONSE Corporation in Detroit, one of the top answering services that I have found. Barbara Kasoff, president of the corporation, says they have been providing services since 1988 to entrepreneurs, many of whom operate from their homes or from one- or two-person shops. "We act as employees or as a message center, depending upon our client's preferences," she says. "The people who call our clients would never believe that they are not talking to an employee at a sophisticated, state-of-the-art corporation."

How can an answering service provide such realism? "By working with the client," Kasoff says. "It's not uncom-

Quick Tips from the Telephone Doctor

NANCY FRIEDMAN, founder and president of Telephone Doctor, has built an international training company by teaching businesses how to use the phone. I asked her to share her top five tips for new small business owners working from their homes:

1 If your budget doesn't allow you to have separate lines for business and home, then answer your home line like a business 100 percent of the time. "Hello" doesn't cut it in a business situation.

2 Teach anyone you live with to do the same thing—kids, parents, spouse, significant other. The phone should be answered in the business mode all the time.

3 If you use an answering machine, make sure the caller knows where you are and when you will return. Callers don't need to know where you are not; they want to know when you will call them back. (Caution: Never use the phrase "We're not home right now.")

4 Keep barking dogs away from your business area. Animal noises won't sound professional at all. Same goes for crying kids, loud TV, and the like. Make sure your office area is in a safe, business-friendly environment.

5 When leaving phone messages for a client, be sure you repeat your phone number twice and slowly. Don't you wish others would do that for you?

The Telephone Doctor offers audios, books, videos, and seminars on customer service and telephone skills. Find them on the Web at www.telephonedoctor.com.

mon for clients to come in to our offices and conduct a training for the staff on how they want phones answered. Some provide scripts. And for distant and international clients who can't visit our office, we hold telephone training conferences and do role-playing until everyone is comfortable and satisfied."

When shopping for an answering service, Kasoff recommends the following:

◆ Determine what your needs are first, then find out if the service can satisfy them. For example, does the service provide both live and automated answering, or a combination, such as business hours live but after-hours and weekends automated? "If that's what you want, it's available," Kasoff confirms.

◆ Check on staffing levels, quality of staff, and the training they receive. At Voice Response, the staff tally fluctuates between eight and thirty, depending on active projects, but all customer service representatives are stable and long-term. Each representative has attended or graduated from college, which Kasoff says tends to aid in professionalism and knowing how to work the calls.

◆ Find out what reporting and communication the service will provide for you. Kasoff says, "We measure all call durations, log time and extensions so clients can determine which media are paying off, record hang-ups and average caller connect time, and develop and manage databases."

◆ Ask what your options are for receiving select calls but letting the service handle the rest. "It's possible to have a service fax or e-mail you immediately or transfer the calls directly to you," Kasoff says. "Still other clients just want a report at the end of each day."

The bottom line, according to Kasoff, is "Don't hire a service until you're completely comfortable. It's important that you determine what you want, then find it, rather than finding a service and settling for what they offer. A good service should not only work with the image you're trying to create but help to develop it, too."

My only other bit of advice would be to check up periodically on the service by calling yourself, and don't hesitate to let them know when performance is good or bad.

MAKE YOUR EFFORTS SERVE DOUBLE DUTY

PRODUCING MARKETING MATERIALS THAT RESULT IN SALES AND IMAGE DEVELOPMENT

WRITING. IT'S SIMPLE, RIGHT? AFTER ALL, WE BEGAN DOING it in kindergarten. Yet most entrepreneurs fall into one of two camps. They either feel unsure about their written messages or don't consider the task important enough to give more than an initial effort. And no wonder: their bailiwick is generally product development, management, or some other specialty that took them into business ownership in the first place. As a result, marketing materials are too often *assumed* to be understood and effective. If they are ineffective and confusing, the impact can hurt not only your image but also your bottom line.

Marketing materials can persuade, inform, and motivate your readers. Done well, they can earn you the respect and credibility you need to advance your company and to build strong relationships with clients. If your materials are poorly written or look cheap, the impression is that your company is not successful, that you may not be around tomorrow, and that you have a small clientele or a limited number of prospects.

Unfortunately, as a small or home-based business entrepreneur, you have to get clients to take you seriously and look upon you as a viable potential contender to fulfill their needs *before* you even get the chance to establish a working relationship (or a sale or contract) with them. What you put in your marketing materials and how you describe your company and its services or products may get you the recognition you want when you can't be there to capture it yourself. If, however, your message is not communicated effectively—for example, your recipient cannot understand it, is not impressed by it, or is not motivated to learn more—then your effort will have been for naught.

Whether you usually write one-page letters and memos

or multiple-page proposals, brochures, or other documents to market yourself, few tasks are as challenging as "putting it in writing" for others to learn from, act upon, or respond to. Yet there is a greater need for effective written material today than ever before; the growth of desktop publishing and associated software, coupled with readily available presentation products and services from retailers such as Kinko's and Staples, have made the business world expect quality materials. This section describes how to use today's technology to produce well-written and well-designed materials that will promote readership; set publications apart from the competition's; and provide organization, unity, and coordination to a business image. And because your written messages should do more than just convey information, this section will present tips on how to use writing to build relationships, sell your ideas, and polish your professional image. What this section will *not* do is concentrate on grammar and basic writing techniques, which are readily available in any standard writing textbook. This specialized section—as with the entire book—is concerned with techniques that have an impact on your company's image and ability to rival the competition.

Keep It Simple

◆ **Be brief.** Keep your letters brief and to the point; you're the head of a successful and busy operation, remember? Besides, your letters stand a better chance of being read if they're short and free of wordy explanations and desperate sales ploys.

There are, of course, challenges to every rule. Herman Holtz, author and specialist in advertising and independent consulting, says that prospects will "read any copy that captures and holds their interest . . .and they won't read copy that doesn't." The implication is that the reader will read long material if he's interested enough. We've all gotten marketing pieces that seem to go on and on. Apparently the companies who send them follow a commissioned study that says the longer the letter, the more likely the recipient will be to purchase whatever it is the company is selling. The objective then is to keep the reader's attention for as long as possible. Don't believe it in the business arena! Long letters may be appealing at home as we relax in front of the tube in the evening and go through the mail looking for that one offer that's going to make us richer, smarter, or thinner. At work, however, the shortage of time, the demands of the job, and the competition all dictate that our material make a point quickly. You're competing with big companies that use either outside marketing firms or layers of management to develop strategic correspondence. Reviewing your writing two or three times to verify clarity and impact are worth the time and effort.

◆ **Write to express, not to impress.** If you write to express, then you *will* impress. Your reader won't be impressed if he can't understand your message. Here are the six most common business writing errors:

1 Passive voice. Use active voice; it gets your point across more powerfully and with fewer words.

PASSIVE
The proposal was drafted by John.

ACTIVE
John drafted the proposal.

2 Wordiness. Unnecessary words clutter your message and can mislead or confuse the reader.

WORDY
We have enclosed the reference manual for the purpose of answering the concerns many employees have in regard to sick-leave policies and procedures.

CONCISE
The enclosed manual covers the company's procedures for sick leave.

3 Negative language. Negative words and expressions generally result in negative responses, or at the least, confuse the reader.

NEGATIVE
If you don't send us the response card within 30 days, we won't be able to register you in time for the seminar.

POSITIVE
Send your response card (more positive) by May 10 (more specific) to secure a position at the seminar.

4 Clichés, jargon, and qualifiers. These phrases can cause confusion and frustration for the reader. Qualifiers often suggest lack of confidence. Use simple, authoritative words.

WIMPY
I'd appreciate it if you would send the check as soon as possible.

CONFIDENT
Please send the check by April 25 to avoid further charges.

5 Stiff tone and style. Make sure your words sound as though they come from a human being—not an institution.

INSTITUTIONAL
Further notification will follow. . . .

HUMAN PERSPECTIVE
I will keep you informed. . . .

6 Use of the "I" perspective. Write from the readers' perspective and they will be more receptive to your message.

"I" PERSPECTIVE
I am unable to handle your request for copies of our brochure at this time.

"YOU" PERSPECTIVE
Thank you for your interest in our services. A brochure is forthcoming; meanwhile, you can. . . .

◆ **Ask your clients.** If you're not sure how to describe yourself in your materials and you can't afford a professional writer or marketing and advertising firm, then turn to trusted clients. Ask them to write testimonials for you that include a description of your services. You might be surprised at how your clients view your company. Happy clients will assume that you want to quote them in your material. . .and yes, smart clients will recognize that this means at least one more place their name may be presented.

◆ **Verify readability.** Always check marketing materials for readability. Either use a reading level calculation or give your material to children who read at the seventh-grade level (the level generally required to be able to read the daily newspaper). Ask the children to tell you in their own words what you have said. Don't use your own children, however; because they live in the same house, they will have a better understanding than other children of the buzzwords and phrases that you use. The exception to the standard readability rule would be if your work is particularly specialized and you must communicate in the jargon of your trade to reach your clients.

◆ **Get feedback.** Once your material has passed the kid test of readability described above, move on to the next testing level: determine if it communicates in the way you intended it to. Does it prompt, inform, incite, motivate as you hoped it would? Give your writing to at least two people (objective people, not friends or family) and ask them to tell you what it says to them and what kind of perception they have about the company that produced it. It will be awkward to ask for this feedback, but so what? It will probably prove to be very insightful.

If you have a business partner or associate, make a pact that neither of you will send anything out the door before the other reads it. My former partner and I did this. As long as you agree to disagree at times, you will find that the review by a second reader results in a tighter and clearer message.

◆ **Don't tell it all.** A well-written marketing piece informs, granted, but if it informs too much, where is the motivation for the recipient to get in touch to learn more about you?

And as you know, it's when you are talking in person that you stand your best chance of enhancing your image, securing a presentation, or making a sale. For example, if you offer a service, you might outline in your brochure the end results of what you will do for a company. However, if you also tell them exactly *how* you will do it, they may be turned off, thinking that you have only one way of providing a service—a way that might not fit into their corporate culture or procedures. If, on the other hand, you leave *how* you carry out the service somewhat vague, they will be more likely to give you a call to learn more. During that call, you will be able to ask questions about the company's mode of operation and then tailor your answers to their situation.

◆ **Go beyond the use of a spell checker and grammar checker.** Most word processing programs feature them nowadays, so there is no excuse for misspelled words, typographical errors, and poor grammar. But don't rely solely on them; read the material yourself, the old-fashioned way. Why? This sentence would pass most spell checker tests: "Eye use a spell chequer on my pea sea."

Keep It Professional

◆ **Go for quality.** Invest in professional marketing materials, whether that investment means outsourcing the job to a graphic designer or putting your money into a good desktop publishing program you can operate yourself. "Marketing materials such as business cards, stationery, and brochures are like little pieces of yourself and your company that you leave behind with a prospective client," says Christina Gimbel, president of Xina Design in Baltimore. "Do you want your client thinking you're unique, polished, professional, and established, or do you want to send the message that you're a slightly modified template?"

If you're a new and financially challenged business, then use a simple typeface on quality paper. Gimbel recommends avoiding the preprinted stationery and brochures found in catalogs and office supply stores. "These products are alright to use if you're just starting your business and it's in an industry that is not visually sophisticated, such as finance, medical, legal, or real estate. Fields such as public relations, marketing, advertising, graphic design, publishing, computer/software/Web page development, architecture, interior design, and other creative endeavors demand professionally designed materials," she advises. "Your business simply won't be able to compete with the more established ones if you've made your own business cards and brochures in the basement. Before your client can even file that card into a Rolodex, the laser-printer toner is fading, and so is the good impression you hoped to make on that prospective client."

◆ **Be consistent.** Gimbel also recommends maintaining a consistent presentation and marketing identity. "Your materials—cards, stationery, brochures, and other marketing pieces—should coordinate," she advises. "A consistent look for your marketing materials will help define you as a focused and established business and will build brand recognition with your clients."

Besides consistency in her marketing pieces, Gimbel places her signature mark, a capital *X*, on all her materials. "I ordered a simple handheld embosser from a stationery supply store," she says. "At first I wondered whether the $80 price tag would be worth the expense, but now I know it was. I get so many positive comments from clients who are impressed when they see my *X* embossed on everything from envelopes to standard manila folders. Embossing the materials myself allows me to create unified packages, even if I use a variety of papers, envelopes, labels, etc."

◆ **Produce several pieces.** Being consistent in theme and presentation of materials doesn't mean that you can't have more than one brochure if you offer more than one product or service. Consider producing a brochure or capability statement for each product or for each target market you serve, since one product or service can serve different clients in different ways. Concentrate on the benefits you provide to each particular type of client; a generic one-fits-all brochure generally cannot sufficiently arouse the desired response.

- ◆ **Keep materials current.** Out-of-date materials imply that you are an out-of-date company. Big companies have in-house printing departments that keep publications updated. You want to create the same impression.

- ◆ **Don't use a résumé.** If you are a consultant and your business is based solely upon the expertise you provide, avoid using a résumé to promote your services. You will have to develop a résumé to satisfy clients, of course, but it can be a detrimental first marketing piece. For example, the client may find fault with the jobs you took when first starting your career or zero in on the college you attended rather than the experience you have attained. A résumé reflects too much what you have been. It's what you are now that you want the client to hire.

Write for More Exposure

- ◆ **Write for your client.** Volunteer to write a regular column or article for your client's newsletter. It's a terrific way to become more entrenched in that organization. If you keep the piece "you" focused rather than "I" focused, the client will probably ask for more, since it means less copy for them to write. And you won't have to sell yourself in the piece, because the company is already a client; what the article does is prolong your tenure with them and enhance your image as a partner in their efforts. You might even ask if your picture can be included with the column. The more recognizable you are to the client's employees, the more you will be perceived as one of their own. This can help to secure more work from them.

- ◆ **Get maximum coverage.** If you decide to try the aforementioned idea, then play it smart: write one article or column and provide it to *all* your clients, provided they are geographically scattered. You can write one piece that, with just a little extra time, can be tailored to each client.

- ◆ **Write your own newsletter or one-pager.** If you can't get the OK from clients to provide material for their newsletters, then write one-page information pieces of your own that you mail out. It's a great way to provide an extra to clients and put your name in front of their eyes again. Be careful calling your piece a newsletter, however; a newsletter implies a regular publishing schedule, and you may not want to lock yourself into that expectation. Keep the information piece professional but informal by putting it on a second-page style of stationery (which, of course, carries your company's name).

◆ **Write a book or booklet.** If you think you have the time and wherewithal, write a booklet in your area of expertise. You can have it professionally and tastefully printed without spending a fortune. Imagine how impressive this booklet will look tucked into a proposal package. This may be the one piece that makes your proposal stand apart from the rest.

◆ **Copyright your materials.** Protecting your writing makes it look valuable. Register booklets, training materials, and other publications with the U.S. Copyright Office, if appropriate. Generally all it takes is $30 and the time to complete a simple one-page form for the Library of Congress. You can receive these forms by calling the Copyright Office hotline any time day or night at 202-707-9100.

Whether you intend them to be or not, the materials you produce may be one of your most valuable assets. Copyrighting your work tells the world that what you produce is important and worth protecting. Under law, most of these materials are considered intellectual property and, like other property you own, can be guarded against theft. Copyright laws help protect written, photographic, and artistic work. The laws state that they protect "original works of authorship that are fixed in a tangible form of expression."

Under U.S. copyright laws, works created on or after March 1, 1989, are automatically copyrighted the moment you place them on a fixed form, such as a paper, book, sheet music, disk, film, audiotape, or some other format that others can read, see, or listen to. This means that works do not have to carry a copyright notice or be registered to be covered by copyright. However, I advise doing both, because putting the notice on your work tells the world not to copy it, and registering the work adds the protection of creating a public record of your registration and ownership. This will validate the copyright in court.

To add a copyright notice, you simply put the copyright symbol ©, the year of publication, and the name of the copyright owner: for example, © 2000 Debra Koontz Traverso.

Other Written Pieces

- ◆ **Print Christmas cards.** Have your Christmas cards specially printed, such as "Happy Holidays from the staff of XYZ International." Then add a personal, handwritten note. You do not want your customers to think that you are too successful to treat them properly. Another idea: if you want to stand apart from the competition by avoiding the sheer volume of cards, skip the Christmas cards and send Thanksgiving (or other holiday) cards instead. Another advantage to Thanksgiving cards is that they can easily be tied to the holiday's purpose—being thankful (for good customers); and your reputation for being a solid, innovative, independent-thinking company is boosted.

  A third idea: send birthday cards. A birthday wish is personal and will have relatively little competition.

- ◆ **Type your envelopes.** Type or laser print the addresses for your envelopes. Do not handwrite them; the impression is that you—or your staff—haven't figured out how to feed envelopes through your laser printer.

- ◆ **Print labels.** Have labels printed for envelopes that are larger than the standard business size. You will need large envelopes, and it's generally very costly to have them custom printed. Read more about preprinted labels on page 164.

- ◆ **Make "Courtesy of" labels.** Buy clear labels that can be fed through your printer. On them, print your company name, address, and phone number beneath the words "Courtesy of." When you come across articles relevant to your business and clients, secure permission from the publication to photocopy and distribute them (generally publications won't charge you for this). Attach one of your preprinted labels and mail them to clients. (Note: Be sure to include the obligatory statement that indicates your permission to copy the article: "Reprinted with permission from . . . .")

◆ **Use stationery slips.** Have small stationery slips printed with your name on them for correspondence that doesn't require a formal cover letter. Most large companies provide note-size slips to executives and some middle managers, so you should have some, too. Avoid using the phrase "From the desk of. . . ." Instead, choose simple stationery notes listing your name, company name and address, and phone number and a brief tag line or description. Don't limit your use of these slips by including your title; your name is sufficient for personalization. The money you save by not using your formal letterhead every time you want to send a message will justify the relatively minor cost of these notes.

◆ **Attach clever notes.** Occasionally when mailing something minor to a client, have your spouse or assistant write on a Post-it note, "Mr. Smith, (your name) asked me to forward this. K" and attach it to the correspondence.

Are You Using Your Tag Line to Full Advantage?

A TAG LINE IS A SLOGAN, CLARIFIER, MANTRA, COMPANY statement, or guiding principle that describes, synopsizes, or helps to create an interest in your company. Examples include Coke: "It's the real thing"; Wal-Mart: "We sell for less"; Marlboro: "Come to where the flavor is"; Nike: "Just do it"; and the *New York Times*: "All the news that's fit to print." A tag line should support your marketing material and provide a cohesive impression of your company's identity, so don't overlook it as a valuable message to use on routine correspondence.

The public wants to know more about you, just as you want to know more about them. They want to know what distinguishes your company from others and how they can benefit from it. The description can be an educational way of giving them that answer. Who could argue the point that Gucci is trying to make with their tag line: "Quality is remembered long after the price is forgotten."

The second reason a tag line can enhance your image is that it helps to develop familiarity with the public through repeated exposure. Familiarity is important because a company with a reputation that is only vaguely familiar has an advantage over one that is completely unknown. Why? Because of a peculiar human trait: a tendency to assign positive attributes to things that are familiar. This is why some companies conduct so much advertising. We've heard "Say it with flowers" from the Society of American Florists so often that we all know to turn to this product as a way of expressing an emotion when mere words will not do. Even more ingenious are tag lines that incorporate the company or product name: "It's a Kodak moment"; "You can be sure if it's Westinghouse"; and "With a name like Smucker's, it has to be good."

A tag line can provide a third, important feature—helping you distinguish yourself from the competition. IBM's slogan? "Think." Not to be outdone, Apple advised, "Think different." My favorite tag line doesn't come from a corporate giant or a technological gadget but rather from an outfit that makes chocolate chip cookies. Their trucks, stationery, and signs all read: "Uncle Ralph's *not yet famous* Cookies." (The *"not yet famous"* always appears in smaller, cursive writing to stand apart from the name.) This powerful statement says that they plan to be famous but recognize that they're not yet. It also implies that they try as hard or harder than the competition. And, of course, there's the allusion to one competitor, Famous Amos cookies, which adds that much more appeal to their tag line. According to Peggy Wight, president of Uncle Ralph's, the tag line "has really worked wonders for us. People remember us, and they are constantly joking with our sales reps and asking, 'Aren't you famous yet?' This gives them the opening to point out that although we distribute to six states and the District of Columbia now, we're not as famous yet as we plan to be." The phrase obviously appeals to a customer's sense of fun. Depending on the nature of your company and product, humor could help you connect with your customers in a positive way. Who could argue with the impact of "Where's the beef?" for Wendy's restaurant or "Sometimes you feel like a nut" for Mounds and Almond Joy candy?

Consider adding your tag line anywhere you feature your company name and logo. It doesn't have to be in large type. In a small font, it can be added to mailing labels, checks, sales slips, office memos, and more.

Finally, put your company name, phone number, and tag line on your product if possible. It only makes good sense to use your product as its own advertisement.

From Vague to Powerful by Changing One Word

IF YOU WANT TO BE CONVINCING, BE AS SPECIFIC IN YOUR writing as possible. Instead of saying "We received numerous inquiries," say, "We received 147 inquiries." Use statistics, numbers, percentages, and examples to support your writing and your claims.

Example: My former partner and I once directed a communication workshop for rocket scientists (literally) and other employees from NASA and the Jet Propulsion Laboratory who were working on the Cassini Project, prior to its launch. At the time, the project represented the world's only fully funded probe to the outer planets—in this case, the planet Saturn. Because the spacecraft was fueled by nuclear power and was scheduled to include an Earth flyby, the mission was plagued with controversy in the news media regarding its safety. We spent two days showing the workshop attendees how to convert their highly technical jargon and risk messages into understandable terms for the layperson. Yet weeks after putting their new knowledge into practice, it was one almost-overlooked bit of advice that they thanked us for the most: before the workshop, they had been referring to the risk of an accident and resulting potential cancer levels in terms of *de minimis* level, saying "one in a million." I advised them instead to say "one in *one* million." While the difference may seem inconsequential, the attendees reported that they were amazed at how many reporters had responded skeptically to the "one in a million" phrase. In contrast, reporters accepted "one in one million" as though it was a scientifically calculated statistic.

The Word That Sells: "You"

WHY WOULD USING THE WORD "YOU" HELP BOLSTER "MY" image? Because you will look customer-focused. Adopting a you-focused strategy is perhaps one of your biggest opportunities to compete with big companies, since along with growth often come complacency and staleness.

The most effective messages are those that personally reach the reader. Emotion causes change. If you can appeal to the emotions of the readers, they will become more receptive to your message. Determine how your product or service will make someone thinner, richer, smarter, kinder, more promotable, more popular, or more organized. *Every* product or service can be linked to someone's emotion, even if the only benefit is that their work becomes easier or it lets them relax, worry-free.

WEAK
Built in a bookshelf-size enclosure, the K113 is designed to be used where floor-standing models cannot be accommodated.

REVISED
If you can't use a floor-standing model, the K113, built for a bookshelf-size enclosure, will solve your organizing problems for you.

See what I mean?

Your Brochure: Not the Place to Cut Costs

YOUR COMPANY WILL NEED AT LEAST ONE MARKETING PIECE that you can mail, distribute, or leave with potential clients. After all, you may not be in your customers' offices or homes when they finally get around to considering your work, but your brochure, flyer, booklet, or catalog can be.

As important as the piece is, it's equally important that it be written and designed well. If you can't afford to do a first-class brochure, wait until you can. An inferior brochure is worse than no brochure at all.

"Too many customers are willing to pay for the design and printing of a brochure but not the writing," says Lori Blake, owner of Image Lab, a full-service design, layout, and printing service in Maryland. "They want to do that themselves. As a result, their writing is not as objective or targeted as it could be."

If you simply must write it yourself, Blake recommends the following:

◆ Start the brochure with brief introductory information about the company and how customers can benefit from your services.

◆ Decide specifically what you expect from the brochure before you proceed. This will help you clarify your message.

◆ Keep it simple and brief. Less is more.

◆ Visualize the audience and write for them. What would your targeted audience want to know about you?

◆ Leave the design and printing to a professional. Your time is best spent running your company, and if you shop around you can find competitive pricing.

If you just can't afford a professional to do the design, try the graphic design program at your local community college. Students are generally hungry for an opportunity to collect real-life experience. Better still, talk to a design professor and see if the brochure could be a group assignment. This way, you'll get several to choose from. Offer a small cash prize for first place, and you'll have the students' complete dedication to the project.

Words That Work

WRITING PROMOTIONAL MATERIAL IS HARD ENOUGH WHEN you're bigger, older, richer, and better known than your competition, but what do you write if you're new and small? Fear not; there are many dynamic ways to describe your company and its services that will make you sound solid and worthy of serious consideration by potential clients. For example, you may not be able to say that your product "has stood the test of time," but you may be able to describe it as "authentic," which elicits the same feeling of comfort. You may not have much "experience" to offer, but no doubt you have "talent" and "imagination." And rather than describing your company as "new," you might say you are "innovative" or "revolutionary."

Below are some descriptive words and phrases to get you started:

◆ **Instead of "older," try:**
—genuine   —the real thing
—true   —the original _____
—the one and only   —actual
—backed by. . .

◆ **Just because your company isn't "big," doesn't mean your scope of services, line of products, or commitment to customer service isn't big. Try these words to suggest size:**
—sizable   —huge
—a feast of. . .   —a gold mine of. . .
—a host of. . .   —a treasure trove of. . .
—a wealth of. . .   —boundless
—substantial   —voluminous
—unlimited   —a multitude of. . .
—multiple. . .

◆ **You may not have offices in every state, which makes you less "convenient" than the competition, but there are other ways to describe your availability and commitment to service:**
—right at your fingertips   —fits your schedule
—accessible   —ready to go anywhere you are
—flexible when it comes   —whenever you want it
  to. . .   —there when you need it
—wherever you need it

◆ If you can't say you're "better known," try:

- distinguished
- prestigious
- accomplished
- noteworthy
- outstanding
- the _____'s choice
- commanding
- flourishing
- in demand
- in vogue
- preferred by more. . .
- approved by. . .
- respected
- premier
- notable
- of high repute
- More and more _____ are discovering _____
- recommended by more. . .
- chosen by. . .
- the area's leading. . .
- word-of-mouth popularity
- endorsed by. . .
- bought by more. . .

◆ If you're new, you probably aren't very "experienced," so try:

- satisfying
- unforgettable
- perfect
- talented
- accomplished
- mastery of. . .
- flair for. . .
- well versed in. . .
- imagination and talent
- got the right stuff
- trained
- gifted
- competent
- _____ is our strong suit
- memorable
- pleasing
- inviting
- qualified
- pioneers in. . .
- talent for. . .
- skilled
- ingenious
- have vision
- entrepreneurial in. . .
- capable
- thoroughly familiar with. . .
- imaginative
- _____ is our specialty

153

◆ Rather than saying you're "new," try:

- innovative
- groundbreaking
- bold
- a fresh approach
- designed for today's _____
- state-of-the-art
- trailblazing
- revolutionary
- latest technology
- for tomorrow's needs
- a revolution in _____

—makes the　　　　　　　—unprecedented
　　　　　 obsolete　　　　—a novel approach

◆ **"Longstanding" and "time-tested"—as used by your competition—sound very inviting, but so does:**
—practical　　　　　　　　—reliable
—reinforced　　　　　　　—laboratory tested
—carefully tested　　　　—complies with. . .
—exceed _____　　　—research shows
　 standards for. . .　　　—dependable
—stands up to. . .　　　　—durable
—functional　　　　　　　—faithful to. . .
—valid　　　　　　　　　—sound
—trusted　　　　　　　　—top credentials
—quality controlled　　　—rigorous standards
—stable　　　　　　　　—secure
—firm　　　　　　　　　—in good standing
—the leader in. . .　　　　—selective
—competitive　　　　　　—discriminating
—the Rolls-Royce of. . .　—You'll be in on. . .
—You'll join a select group
　 of. . .

◆ **If you don't have impressive numbers and percentages to prove your claims, then stick with adjectives that will describe the expected results:**
—makes the difference　　—You can count on. . .
—prevents　　　　　　　—reduces
—raises　　　　　　　　—lowers
—cuts down on. . .　　　—revitalizes
—restores　　　　　　　—maintains
—provides　　　　　　　—improves
—never lets up　　　　　—produces
—delivers　　　　　　　—cuts through. . .

◆ **Be sure to include descriptions in your marketing materials that will enhance your image, build your reputation, and set you apart from the competition:**
—Our total commitment to. . .

—We believe in. . .

—We uncover. . .

—We serve. . .

—We uphold. . .

—We honor. . .

—We're dedicated to. . .

—We demand excellence.

—Here are just a few of our clients:

—You are the one who benefits.

—We offer the added advantage of. . .

—Who you buy from can be just as important as what you buy. Here's why:

—We don't play games when it comes to. . .

—our distinctive style of. . .

—our dedication to. . .

—Don't be taken in by. . .

—Don't fall for. . .

—Don't settle for second best. We offer. . .

—Nobody can match our prices/service.

—Unlike other _____, we. . .

—No other _____ comes close to. . .

—We give you more _____ than any other _____

CHANGE MUNDANE TASKS INTO IMAGE-BUILDING ACTIONS

TURNING ROUTINE TASKS INTO VALUABLE CHANCES TO MAKE A STATEMENT ABOUT YOUR COMPANY

THAT STANDARD INVOICE YOU ROBOTICALLY SEND OUT AFTER you've completed a job or a sale should carry through on the same message and impressions that you were so careful to deliver in your first sales letter. This section will discuss how to turn routine tasks like that into valuable chances to make a statement about your business.

You may recall from Chapter 1 that your company's

image is composed of all the planned *and* unplanned verbal and visual impressions on the recipient. If you spend time and money on your *planned* marketing messages but pay little attention to the other correspondence and communication that leaves your office, you are missing valuable opportunities to make powerful, no- to low-cost statements about your company. Included among these unplanned opportunities are purchase orders, mailing labels, telephone messages, references to your company, and the quality of your cellular phone. It may be these and other materials and messages that speak loudest about your size, success, abilities, and attention to details. These messages can project or mumble, clarify or confuse, stimulate or annoy, promote or discourage, support or dissuade, and encourage a sale or fail to motivate at all. In this section, you will learn how to make everything that emanates from your office—from questionnaires to fax cover pages, from checks to voice messages— a purposeful statement supporting the image you wish to present.

Paying attention to every message means that you will need to take a hard look at your electronic presence. Are your machines and gadgets presenting you in the appropriate manner? Are they sending the message you want to convey? These days, anything other than an impressive electronic presence is a clear signal that you are small and behind the times. The appropriate electronic peripherals can actually help to improve a client's otherwise mediocre impression of you.

What you will *not* find in this chapter is a rundown of the latest office equipment, particularly hardware and software options. As has been mentioned earlier, no book can adequately discuss the latest in computer technology. The only way you can be sure you are considering the latest technological advancements for your office is to do your research: visit your local computer stores, search for answers on the Web, and place telephone calls to hardware and software companies you respect, asking pointed questions about what's available and what works.

Finally, this chapter closes with tips to enhance routine

presentation and verbal messages, and an Eighteen-Point Quality Message Assessment that you can apply to every verbal and visual signal associated with your company.

No More Standard Letters

THIS CHAPTER HAS ALREADY DISCUSSED HOW TO PRODUCE dynamic letters and marketing material. Now let's add some details to that correspondence.

◆ **List your board members.** Remember the board of advisers discussed in Chapter 2? Consider listing them on your stationery. The right board of advisers can heighten your image; after all, they can be as involved or cosmetic as you, your image, and your business needs dictate. Sometimes just printing the names of advisory board members on company literature can change a company's image from risky to stable, from questionable to capable. I have seen this done graphically very well. Find someone else's stationery that lists a board of directors on the left side and decide for yourself if it suggests influence, size, success, and stability.

◆ **Add details to letters.** One successful personnel recruiter who worked solo from her home added initials to the bottom left side of her letters suggesting that someone else had typed them for her. Although she made up initials, your best bet is to use initials that stand for something you can easily remember, such as "sfn": stands for nobody; "tmo": type my own; or "tbs": typed by spouse. Before those initials, be sure to add your initials in uppercase; for example, JAS:sfn.

Is this deceptive? Not if your main reason for doing so is to stay organized. Another young entrepreneur I know uses the initials JRT:otr and JRT:imo. He says this helps him distinguish the letters that he writes "on the road" from those he types "in my office." For those who never ask about it, he feels he adds "some implied staffing" to his image; for those who do ask, he uses it as the opportunity to segue to the fact that he has clients throughout the country. In fact, he says he wishes more clients would ask, because those who do would otherwise not know his clientele is so widespread.

◆ **Use a "cc:".** Under "cc:" on all letters, add a name for the destination of the file that indicates an extensive, organized filing system, such as "Invoice File 23F." (If you work from a small office for very long, your cabinets, extra milk crates, and cardboard boxes may indeed need to be labeled if you want to stay organized.) Or add names of people or departments (or filing cabinets) in your office to receive copies of the correspondence.

◆ **Add a well-worded P.S. to letters.** This technique shows cleverness if you attach a postscript that adds something to the letter but doesn't look like an afterthought, even though the definition of a postscript is a message added after the signature. With today's cut-and-paste conveniences on computers, it's obvious that if you chose not to add the material in the body of the letter, it's because you purposely wanted to make it stand out as a P.S. For this reason most postscripts are read by the recipient, even if the rest of the letter is ignored. Therefore, make sure the P.S. is clever and augments the information in the body of the letter, prompting the reader to go back and read the whole thing.

◆ **Add a handwritten note.** When preparing a sales letter that you think may not be read despite your most dynamic writing exertions, consider adding a handwritten note in the margin or a P.S. that cannot stand alone. Adding a message that depends on the context forces the reader to go back and read the entire letter to grasp your meaning. Example: "Smith Hardware trimmed its customer returns 27 percent by using this technique."

◆ **Add a description of your business.** Include a tag line, brief mission statement, or description of your company (ten words or less) at the bottom of your stationery in an italic or coordinating font. If you opted not to add it when the stationery was printed, now is your chance to tailor a tag line to the client you're writing to. It doesn't matter if the tag line is now in black ink, especially if you included black in the stationery design and you use a quality laser printer. Through my former company I offered services in crisis management and crisis communication. Depending upon the client that I was writing to, I would include a tag line at the bottom of the page that addressed his interest, such as the following:

—Nationally known specialists in crisis communication

—Leaders in crisis management plans for the chemical (or whatever) industry

—Conductor of more than 300 on-camera media response training programs

Now I add descriptions that reflect the more recent work I've been doing:

—Humor columnist: *Mind Your Home Business*

—Author—Journalist—Lecturer—Consultant

Provide Information on Your Forms; Don't Just Collect It

◆ **Use your logo.** Imprint your forms, such as invoices and questionnaires, with your business name and logo. If you have a tag line or description, such as "Creative and Confidential Personal Shoppers," "Number one in the mid-Atlantic region," or "Winner of *Boston* magazine's coveted Counselor of the Year Award," repeat it on the business forms.

◆ **Use tracking and revision numbers.** Give each form a four-digit tracking number, printed in a small font in the bottom right corner. Large companies have a multitude of forms; four digits or more suggest that you are large enough to have a lot of forms, too. Use the numbers to help stay organized; you may indeed one day be large enough to require multiple digits to keep track of your forms.

Also, as you develop your forms, you'll probably create a few drafts before producing the final copies. Keep track of how many drafts you produce, then add that number to your final forms; for example, use wording such as "Rev. 3." Besides ease of reference, the number suggests the form has been around a while and has been developed through experience.

◆ **Ensure that faxed forms are legible at the receiving end.** When I was compiling notes for this book, I remembered my friend Allen, who provides career counseling from his home. Allen mails or faxes a form to potential clients when they first call for information, so I asked him to fax one to me. His form featured reverse type and fonts of varying sizes, including a cursive 7-point font. Despite the quality of my fax machine, the form looked like a blur. No one had ever brought this faux pas to his attention.

◆ **Use "Company use only."** On forms and questionnaires that will be returned by clients, leave room (or a box) for "Company use only." The implication is that these forms are going to be read by many people, will be used to record in-house information, and will be kept on file for reference. Your company will appear larger and better organized, because that blank space suggests you've learned from experience and this area serves an important purpose in-house. And, no doubt, you will find that you ought to make notes on that form anyway.

Make That New Checking Account Look Aged and Proven

ESTABLISH A CHECKING ACCOUNT SEPARATE FROM YOUR HOME account. Not only are personal checks a clear sign of your company's size and youth, but mixing business and home accounts will cause confusion at tax time. And while you're ordering, consider these tips:

◆ Use the larger business checks rather than the smaller personal ones. They look more professional, and they fit into standard-size business envelopes better.

◆ Don't order checks with cutesy pictures on them, no matter how much you like Mount Rushmore, cats, or the ocean. If you want your checks to say something about you, then add a tag line or description, not a picture that has nothing to do with your business.

◆ Order checks with your business name and logo on them. You don't have to buy the expensive checks that banks offer. Instead, order them from stationery supply stores or discount check-printing companies, then use the extra money you save to have your logo imprinted on the checks, too.

◆ Start with high numbers on your checks and invoices. Any number below 1,000 is a dead giveaway that you are small or new. I do this on my home accounts, too; I have had my share of raised eyebrows from clerks who have noticed the number 101 after I've opened a new account.

◆ Use software that prints check information, such as payee, date, amount. This is also an efficiency item, since such software can track expenses, monitor sales, and generate all kinds of reports and analyses. The look is very professional. Note that even discount check-printing companies offer a variety of forms that work with computers and special printers.

Don't Overlook Payments

◆ **Direct your payments.** Take a look at the next invoice that you know is from a large company. Notice that they provide you with a specific destination or department to which you are to mail your payment. You should do the same. On your invoices, write: "Please send payment to our Accounting Department at. . . .," or simply add Dept. C-10 (or whatever combination you choose) to the address. Better still, come up with a designation that you can tie into your filing system; the effort of listing a receiving department may as well help to keep you organized, too.

Likewise, on your purchase orders, write: "Please send your invoice to our Purchasing Department at. . . .," so that you can maintain your image when dealing with suppliers. You should treat them with the same care and caution that you give your clients. Although they are profiting from the arrangement, too, and they need your business, they may not be treating you fairly financially if they believe you are a here-today-and-gone-tomorrow operation. I have seen suppliers charge higher rates because they perceived a higher risk when signing on with small companies.

◆ **Record expenses carefully.** When you are working under a time-and-materials contract, you may have to submit your expenses directly to the client. This means that diligent clients might be reviewing everything you did in your hotel room, from whom you called to the movies you watched. Think twice about anything that will be listed on your hotel bill. If you must push the limit on activities in the hotel, then upon check-in discuss the possibility of receiving two bills when you check out. Also, note that I have seen hotels charge as much as $1.75 for access for each local and 800 call. Find out what you will be able to afford, and what you will be able to bill to a client, *before* it's added to the bill.

◆ **Don't nickel-and-dime your clients.** Don't put excessive small charges on invoices for expense items such as photocopies, postage, and telephone calls. This makes you look tight, insecure, and overly concerned about each penny you're owed. When these items are sizable, such as large quantities of booklets, mass mailings, or long phone campaigns, it's acceptable.

Beware the Fax Machine

◆ **Watch the timing of documents you fax.** Generally, they will be stamped with a time at the receiving end. Ask yourself, if you worked outside of your home for a very large employer, would you be faxing at 10 P.M.? Some fax machines and software have a "delay send" feature that will program your fax to be sent late at night when telephone rates are cheaper. You will have to evaluate whether the savings in telephone charges is worth the mental note that clients might make of the fact that you are apparently working after midnight.

◆ **Set up a separate fax line.** Keep it separate from your phone line. Otherwise, your clients will generally have to make two calls: the first one to let you know that they want to fax something; the second to actually fax it. Better still, take advantage of voice messaging that will give callers the option of leaving a message or sending a fax.

◆ **Direct incoming faxes.** Tell anyone faxing to you to be sure to address the material to you. This effort makes it sound as though many people share your office fax machine or the machine is very busy. And after all, it's true. Even if your office has only two or three people, the material is coming to you.

◆ **Don't overdo faxing.** Do not fax to a client from your computer unannounced or unsolicited. Fax messages tie up clients' telephone lines and use their paper.

- **Suppress fax headings if necessary.** If you don't have a fax machine, be cautious when using someone else's. Some fax service providers put their name and logo at the top of faxes they send for you. It doesn't look good if you send a fax that says "Joe's Fax and Deli." Request that the provider suppress that heading if possible.

Use Updated Computer Equipment and Associated Support

THE RIGHT EQUIPMENT AND AFFILIATED SUPPORT DEPEND ON your unique business needs, brand preference, and budget, so shop wisely and evaluate your options by how useful they would be. For example, when buying a computer, look for a model that comes bundled with business software like office suites and financial management programs, as opposed to consumer models that feature unnecessary video and audio cards and speakers. A PC can do more than just boost office productivity—it has the secondary use and effect of helping to improve your image, to organize your many tasks, to provide faster service to customers, and to keep you on schedule. Finally, scrutinize the type of warranty and support offered; you'll be glad you did when you need help. Keep these tips in mind when it comes to your equipment and support:

163

- **Keep software updated.** Use the most common and latest versions of computer software. Become familiar with what your clients use. It can prove embarrassing if you have to announce to a client that you can't work with material he gives you because you have an out-of-date version.
- **Protect your computer system.** Use antivirus software. Always scan disks received from other people. It's hard to explain to a client that you lost files. Yes, even large and successful companies occasionally have computer virus problems. But do you want to detract from your image of efficiency and success by having these situations occur?
- **Don't lose your e-mail.** Make sure your e-mail (outgoing and incoming) does not get cut off when a telephone call comes in.

- **Buy a quality printer.** Get one that will produce the most professional image you can afford. Do not use a dot-matrix printer. Invest in a laser printer with a resolution of at least 600 dots per inch.
- **Back up critical files.** Establish a routine for backing up your computer files. Stay away from tape drives (too unreliable) and from floppies (too inconvenient). Instead, try an external device like Iomega's Zip and Jaz drives, a recordable CD-ROM drive, or off-site online backup services.
- **Store computer backup disks in a safe place.** Keep them separate from your home office, in case of vandalism or fire. A client's impression of your reliability may suffer if you lose a file they need; after all, this seldom happens at large organizations, due to their system setup. A safe deposit box at your local bank is an inexpensive yet effective way to store your backup floppies, tapes, or Zip drives, although it doesn't offer after-hours access. Or try an online data-storage company (search the Internet using "online data storage" as a locating term). Even less expensive is keeping copies at a relative's or friend's house, or at your spouse's or buddy's office.

Don't Overlook Your Mail

- **Use preprinted envelope labels.** Have labels preprinted if your work involves sending out proposals and capabilities summaries or any other material that requires envelopes larger than the standard business size. It's costly to have large envelopes custom-printed, whereas labels are versatile, and you can buy many inexpensive ones that work in a laser printer. Use them on envelopes that are marked first class. Your clients will think you used such an envelope because your first priority was to ensure first-class transport; they won't assume it was because you were trying to save money. Besides, the custom-printed labels add the touch of unity and quality to your written material that custom-printed envelopes would have provided.
- **Lease a postage meter with a scale.** This will save you time (and money during hurried situations), and for an addi-

tional fee, some postage meters will print your company's name and logo in the meter area.

◆ **Send correspondence in separate envelopes.** Large companies do not coordinate correspondence from separate departments prior to mailing something; thus, the implication will be that the two pieces of mail came from different people or departments in your company.

◆ **Establish overnight delivery accounts.** Set up accounts with service providers such as UPS and Federal Express. These accounts generally do not cost you anything, and they provide your business with preprinted (with your company name and address) shipping labels. This looks more impressive than handwritten, generic shipping forms.

Or get software from the overnight delivery service providers. This software can generate the paperwork, print your shipping forms, register the shipment, and track all your deliveries. Custom shipping forms look like you use these services often and thus are successful. Additionally, you can track any of your shipments on your computer.

◆ **Advertise on your business envelopes.** Yes, I'm talking about the standard 4" x 9$^{1}/_{2}$" envelope that has your return address printed in the upper left corner. Ever notice that when you get your bills, particularly from department stores, the envelope features lots of advertising on it? That's because smart advertisers know that between the time the envelope leaves the business and it reaches you, it will pass through a lot of hands. . . and pass by a lot of eyes. I'm not suggesting you adulterate your envelopes with all sorts of colors and font sizes; keep it professional. For example, add your tag line or other message on the bottom left corner or other prime spot on the envelope. I once got a bill from a plumber who had printed on the back of the envelope (which is the side everyone holds toward them as they attempt to open the seal) "This otherwise wasted spot gives us the opportunity to say thank you for the privilege of serving you." Sure, it's a little wordy, but I'd rather my plumber be earnest, clever, and resourceful than pithy and articulate. His use and placement of the message impressed me, so he was the one I called the next time I needed help.

And Don't Forget Your Product!

LET'S FACE IT: THE BIG GUYS ARE EASY TO TRACK DOWN AND find in the yellow pages or on the Web. So make yourself easy to locate and contact: put your company name, phone number, and tag line on your product if possible. It only makes good sense to use your product as its own advertisement. I learned this good practice from Landers hand cream. Years ago, in pre-Web days, my mother swore by Landers, saying it was the only hand cream that gave her relief from sore skin. Suddenly one day she could no longer find it on store shelves. We searched for months in local stores and called all the relatives to search in their hometowns. My mother was prepared to order a case of the cream. Unfortunately, the empty jar had no address or phone number. We never found it again.

This advice applies even if you provide a service rather than a product. I have gone into countless training sessions for clients to find that—without my knowing—a guest from a neighboring company or even a competitor had been invited to observe from the back of the room. Fortunately, because my company's name and phone number are included on all distributed training materials, those companies were able to—and did!—get in touch with me.

There are exceptions to this rule, too, however. If you offer a product through retail stores, you may find that those stores won't want customers to be able to bypass them to go directly to the source. Thus, they may not allow your phone number to be printed on the product. Solution? Put your name and city on your label: Michael's Furniture/Boston. Interested buyers can still locate you through telephone directories and Internet services.

Scrutinize Everything That Goes Out Your Door

BELOW IS A LIST OF ITEMS THAT MIGHT BE USED IN YOUR BUSiness. Ask yourself: Are you taking advantage of every opportunity to market and establish the appropriate image on these routine pieces? Can you be contacted through each of these pieces?

◆ **Typical marketing pieces**

—letterhead
—business cards
—capability summary
—catalog covers
—advertisements

—second-page stationery
—news releases
—service brochures
—sales bulletins and flyers
—direct mail pieces

◆ **Atypical marketing pieces**

—statements
—envelopes
—catalog pages
—purchase order forms
—shipping papers
—annual/quarterly reports
—packaging materials
—giveaways
—sales slips
—cartons
—training manuals
—tape
—vehicle decals and stickers

—acknowledgments
—name and address change
  mailers
—office memos
—mailing labels
—shipping containers
—wrapping paper
—checks
—paper and plastic bags
—gift boxes
—cloth labels
—decals

Business Cards—Get Creative

MORE THAN 35 MILLION BUSINESS CARDS ARE EXCHANGED each day; hand yours out generously. Large companies often print cards in-house, so restocking supplies is not a concern; don't make it look like a concern for you, either. Then again, give your card value by not handing it out too eagerly. The impression then is that you're either hungry for fame or desperate for sales. Get a sense of whether or not you want someone to be able to locate you before you hand out a card.

◆ Keep business cards available. Put some in your wallet or purse, coat pockets, glove compartment, and briefcase. Fumbling around to find a card suggests that you don't hand them out very often. You want to project the image that people ask you for your card often; therefore, you know where you keep them.

◆ Always hand out a card to anyone who must leave before a meeting or luncheon ends. This gives you an opportunity to ask for their card. Later, you can send a note to them telling them that you enjoyed meeting them and, if appropriate, summarize what they missed. The point here is to look helpful and thoughtful, not overly eager to market.

◆ When someone asks you for a recommendation, write the information on the back of your card if the answer is short. What's your favorite restaurant? Write it on the back of a card. Can you give directions to XYZ Corporation? Draw the directions on the back of a card. Again, use this tactic if the person you're talking to is someone you want to be able to locate you. Otherwise, use a slip of paper.

◆ Have a second set of business cards printed; on them, give yourself a demotion. Instead of being president or CEO, introduce yourself as Managing Director or Director of Operations or Marketing. You will have to determine what will work best for you and each client. Some clients merit a president calling on them the first time; others will wonder how a supposedly busy and successful company can afford to send the president out on routine calls. Still others may be more candid about business opportunities with a sales manager than with a company CEO. You can sometimes avoid awkwardness later on by forgoing a title and simply listing a function, such as Marketing or Strategic Development.

◆ Occasionally you'll meet someone or hear of someone who may be able to use your business, but you have no formal way of getting your card in their hands. When this happens, watch for news articles or other materials that may interest them. Attach your business card to the material with a paper clip, with your name and company turned toward the material. On the back of the card, write a brief note such as "Thought you might like this since it pertains to your business."

◆ Since cards are relatively inexpensive, consider having several variations printed if you have several lines of products. Feature a picture of each product on its own card. One home entrepreneur I met, who developed and manufactured several statue-type caricatures for professionals, did this. When he spoke at meetings for engineers, he handed out cards featuring a picture of the engineer caricature. Likewise, when he talked with a group of nurses, he handed out nurse caricatures. Of course his name, company, address, phone number, and e-mail address were included on the cards.

◆ Consider having another set of cards printed in the shape of Rolodex inserts. Clients will be able to snap them directly into their card files without having to take the extra step of taping the cards to a Rolodex insert. The impression will be that you are making their work just a little bit easier; besides, there's a better chance your card will be kept and placed in the Rolodex than if you give them more work to do. Generally these cards are sent, not handed out. A word of caution:

One Extra Effort Can Make the Difference

ADELE SUMMERS, who operates Keeping Current, a bookkeeping business, from her home in Atlanta, likes to take the task of scheduling appointments with potential customers a step beyond routine. After she schedules a meeting and hangs up the phone, she immediately fills out an appointment card. This card is an inexpensive piece that she designed and had professionally printed. The tasteful cards state simply, "I'm looking forward to meeting with you on. . .," then it features blank lines for filling in the day, date, and time.

In addition to displaying her company name, address, phone number, and Web site, it offers a blank space for her to write any message she chooses. Quite often the message she pens will suggest that the client should feel free to call her references or to check her Web site before the meeting. She says she gets positive reactions from clients, who seem impressed with the cards and her thoroughness, and she has noticed that fewer appointments are canceled as a result.

only send this type of card if you think that the client uses such a card filing system. This type of card will not fit into most other filing formats and will just prove to be an irritation for the recipient.

Drop the Routine Mailings

YOU HAVE A GOOD PRODUCT THAT YOU *KNOW* THE XYZ CORporation would just love to buy—once they learn about it, that is. So what do you do? Routine procedure would be to package it professionally, address it to the appropriate recipient, drop it in the mail, and prepare to meet the company's buyer, right?

Wrong, according to Kim Gosselin, president of JayJo Books, a publisher of children's health education books: "If you do that, you'll wait forever for a response."

Kim says you have to be creative and be willing to break from the routine. "There are four problems with a routine mailing. First, it shows no creativity. Second, the package may not get opened for a couple of weeks. Third, it could be opened by somebody other than your targeted contact. And fourth, a standard mailing will not make your product stand out from the many others the company receives, all of which arrive in similar packaging."

Kim's solution is to make her initial contact with overnight mail. She has sold more than $2 million (wholesale) of books to corporations as premiums using this technique.

After she researches the corporation's product and identifies a unique hook to make her product fit theirs, she gets creative. "My first book was a story about a child who is the only one in his classroom suffering from diabetes," Kim explains. "Large publishing houses were not interested, telling me that the book had no market. But I knew it did, so I decided to publish it on my own if I could find help with funding. I reasoned that since pharmaceutical companies sell drugs for diabetes, they might have an interest in seeing the book published. So after thoroughly researching my target companies and finishing a rough prototype of the book, I put the book in a clear children's backpack I found at Wal-

Mart. I also added papers and pencils to make it look like a backpack that was filled for school. Then I packaged it professionally in a box with my proposal and mailed it overnight. Within one week, I was invited to make a presentation in person." That presentation resulted in an impressive sale, and her company was born.

Kim attributes her success to her creative packaging and the fact that an overnight mailing always gets attention. "My contacts are marketing directors. They tend to get a lot of standard envelopes from people hoping to sell them products. Those envelopes get tossed on a pile. But an overnight package suggests importance, quality, and value. People tend to open those packages immediately."

Of course, overnight mail can quickly add up, so you will have to evaluate for yourself whether the cost is worth it. Even if you determine that overnight mail is not practical, Kim's suggestion for presenting your product creatively might be just the boost it needs to stand out from its competitors. Her techniques have sparked enough interest from business owners that she's begun offering consulting services for special and premium sales. She can be reached at jayjobooks@AOL.com.

If Creative Doesn't Work, Try Clever

DO YOU FIND THE ROUTINE TASK OF TRYING TO ESTABLISH new business and getting your foot in the door a little bewildering? I once met a home-based advertising specialist who said he was having so much trouble getting established that he chose the client he most wanted to do work with and mailed him a package. (The client, by the way, had once told him that he didn't think one-person businesses could be very reliable or creative since they had no staff.) So what was in the package? A shoe. Attached to the shoe was a note that read, "Now that I have my foot in the door, can we talk about the creative things I can do for your company?" The shoe worked. The owner was so impressed that he called immediately and scheduled an appointment.

If you don't find such creative techniques quite your style, then opt for clever. Randy S., president of a franchise for a well-known motivational speaking organization, says that when he wants to get his foot inside the offices of a new organization, he does his homework. He identifies the top five executives at the company and writes them each the same letter. In the letter, he tells each recipient who else he is writing to at the organization. He ends the letter by asking

Eighteen-Point Quality Message Assessment

AS EVIDENCED BY this chapter, there are many routine tasks and messages you produce and distribute each day that provide a valuable opportunity to establish your image. Get in the habit of assessing your output by reviewing the questions below. Before long, the assessment will become second nature when you're creating, marketing, talking, and demonstrating. For each task or message you produce, ask yourself if it promotes or stifles the image that your company:

1 Is visible, accessible, and approachable
2 Is well managed
3 Is innovative
4 Provides quality products or services
5 Is reliable
6 Never compromises on fees, advice, service, or principles
7 Is committed to satisfying the customer
8 Is well positioned in a promising industry
9 Keeps abreast of changes in the industry
10 Is financially sound
11 Demonstrates wise use of corporate assets
12 Shows respect and assigns value to a client's assets
13 Is always striving to improve, to offer more
14 Is knowledgeable of competitors' pricing and services
15 Is concerned with ecology
16 Practices good safety habits
17 Demonstrates fair play in dealing with competition
18 Has a good reputation in the area and in the industry

which person he should contact to finalize the day and time for the meeting. Randy claims that nine times out of ten, the recipients are either so impressed with his chutzpah and research or so comfortable assuming that one of their colleagues contacted Randy that they go along with the scheduling of the appointment.

Marketing for Optimum Impact

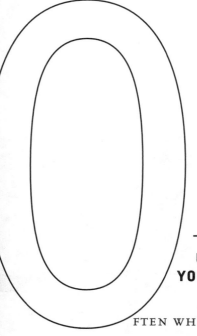

POSITION YOURSELF AGAINST THE COMPETITION

UNIFYING YOUR IMAGE WITH YOUR UNIQUE MARKETING NICHE

FTEN WHEN I'M LECTURING OR HELPING A client, I am asked if it's really possible for small businesses to compete with corporate behemoths. The answer is yes! I've done it. Then the question becomes, how would I have helped Meg Ryan save her too-charming-for-words New York City bookstore against Tom Hanks's humongous book superstore in the movie *You've Got Mail?*

Although the movie was fiction, the real-life equivalent of Ryan's bookstore (upon which the shop in the story was based) is alive and well: Manhattan's Books of Wonder. Meg Ryan even learned how to open and close the gate to the storefront and use a cash register there.

Today the shop is not just surviving, but thriving. A *Forbes* article (January 1999) reported that when a Barnes & Noble opened just four blocks away in 1994, "sales at Wonder leapt by 20 percent." Today there are three Barnes & Noble bookstores within Books of Wonder's marketing area.

How does Books of Wonder compete against an impressive, larger-selection, lower-priced chain operation like Barnes & Noble? I interviewed its manager, Jennifer Lavonier, to find out. The answer, not surprisingly, is that the store is positioned well. It has something to offer that its bigger competition doesn't. Jennifer explains: "You have to provide something more special than a 10 percent discount in my business to survive." She refers to her shop's unique selling feature as "extreme book knowledge."

"When our customers need help in locating or picking a specific book, they know they can come to us. Often people come in with very limited information, and just by saying 'It's a book about a hermit crab who's a pack rat' we know they mean *Kermit the Hermit,* by Bill Peet. We can also suggest titles for specific situations. For example, a four-year-old being bullied at school would appreciate *Hooway for Wodney Wat,* by Helen Lester and Lynn Munsinger. Customers see us as a very service related store because of my knowledgeable staff. It's that kind of specialized service that has kept us in business."

One of her staff's chief forms of promotion is taking their book knowledge to local schools. "We have several teachers who shop here. We plan special events for them and let them know when we're having another signing or presentation," Jennifer says.

Books of Wonder flourishes by offering something the larger Barnes & Noble bookstores do not: specialized customer service. This is their second unique selling proposition or unique selling point (USP in marketing jargon).

Of course, trading on your uniqueness suggests that other pertinent factors between you and your competitors—such as price and selection—are pretty much equal. If your products carry rock-bottom prices yet still provide the quality that your competition's products do, then you have a unique selling feature right there. Aggressive pricing can be one of your best techniques for luring customers away from bigger competitors, especially for large-ticket products. (Lower prices for services, however, may make customers pause to wonder if the service will be as good.) However, you'd have to lower your markup below the industry standard and lower your prices accordingly, and apart from occasional loss leaders, your prices can't be set solely to beat the competition. More often, you'll need to set competitive prices, then support your promotional plans with niche marketing efforts.

Fortunately, every business can be best at something. If you're having trouble determining how you differ, this chapter can help. I'm going to share nine ways in which you can zero in on your niche or USP and differentiate yourself enough to add the value it will take to win the sale.

As you review these nine, remember that what you're trying to do is to locate a niche that matches customer needs (or wants) with your unique selling features for the area(s) in which you can excel. Your USP will require that you position that image in the minds of your prospects. A visible, purposeful difference in benefits must be so obvious to customers that it compels them to buy from you rather than from your competition. Your USP will be the one feature you emphasize that makes you unique. Be sure it's based on truth, that it actually is a strength, and that it's something you can live with for years to come.

Consistency is key. Too many business owners identify their niche, start promoting it, and then weeks or months later become bored or frustrated, thinking that it's not working. You can't change your marketing approach with every change in seasons. Instead, you have to make your marketing efforts work with the seasons. More about that later. For now, as you read the nine items, remember that you are going to develop a winning marketing approach and stick with it. That's one of the reasons I recommend not relying solely on item number one (product or service). Differentiating yourself from the competition in today's marketplace can rarely be done on product or service alone, which provides competitive advantage only until someone else clones it.

Keep this customer-focused question in mind: "Why should I, your potential customer, do business with you, above all other options, including doing nothing?" If you can answer this question with one (or more) of the nine areas, then those techniques should work for you.

Nine Ways to Discover Your Niche

1 **Product or service.** Determine whether your product is unique. What are its quality, features, and reliability compared to similar products on the market? Is it better built, more reliable, or less likely to break? If your price is high-

er, does your product offer more features to merit the increased cost?

Or determine whether your service is unique. What service do you offer that's more reliable or usable by customers? Do customers have a clear understanding of the benefits they'll derive from your service?

An example of being the *only* one to produce a product is artist Pat Merenko Smith, whose Revelation Productions in North Huntingdon, Pennsylvania, creates one-of-a-kind visuals from the biblical book of Revelation. Her artwork from her Revelation Illustrated series is licensed by more than fifty large and small publishers and ministries and sells in sixteen countries.

Like Pat, I pioneered in a business, too, but with a service: crisis management. For a while, the mere fact that we were specialists in helping companies survive and manage crises was enough to bring in consistent work. Before long, however, we began to encounter competition. Fortunately, we had not relied solely on the uniqueness of our service. By the time we had significant competitors, we were able to take advantage of our stability and leadership (item number nine) because we had years of experience under our belt, which also meant that we had more information and expertise (item number two) to offer. Additionally, we delivered excellent customer service (item number eight), and our delivery (item number three) was always on time and within budget. Among these attributes, we chose to highlight one feature more than the others: information (see the next item), based on expertise we had attained in dealing with the news media during times of crisis and in helping companies prepare for the inevitable media onslaught. In fact, I had fine-tuned my expertise so well that even though I've closed my former company, I still share the information about crisis management and communicating with the news media through lectures to students at Harvard University.

2 Information and expertise. Your customers and clients want more than a good product or service. With it they want solutions, information, insights, awareness. If you are the one who has the facts they need, your chances of getting their business have just improved.

Ways to capitalize on information include distributing newsletters, offering free informational seminars, and serving as a convener and a referral point. If you know something worked for one customer, get permission to pass that information along to other customers.

Information can be put in many unusual packages. For example, most of us have seen the movie *Miracle on 34th Street*. In this 1947 family classic, the spirit of Christmas is rekindled in a young girl by an endearing department store Santa who causes a furor when he claims to be the real Kris Kringle. Savvy marketers who watch the movie tend to chuckle at the shocked store owners' reactions when the Macy's Santa tells customers to shop also at Bloomingdale's. That's because marketers have learned to exploit the benefits of positioning their companies and clients as good guys, of serving in the public's interest, of acknowledging to the public any less-than-positive aspects of their product, and of making up for any perceived shortcomings through education and outreach.

3 **Distribution and delivery.** Do you offer home delivery of your product? Is your product distributed in more areas than your competition's? Do you provide unusual gift wrapping with delivery? Do you know if your distribution costs undercut those of your competitors? Can you provide updates on where a customer's order stands, or will customers just have to sweat until the items arrive? If you distribute or deliver your product differently than anyone else does (for example, against aggressive schedules or for less money than the competition), then this may be your niche.

This unique selling proposition does not have to apply to products only. For example, at a home show recently, I graciously accepted anything that was placed in my hand by the hundreds of vendors and dutifully dropped it in my bag. When I got home, I sorted through the bag and noticed that I got cards from four plumbers. The front of the cards looked average, but on the back of one was printed: "When you use other plumbers you will probably get a year's guarantee, at best. When you use me, you get a lifetime unlimited warranty with guaranteed twenty-four-hour service."

I was intrigued enough by this message to call the other three plumbers to find out what *their* guarantees were. I now have the card of the service-delivery-oriented plumber on my refrigerator, awaiting my first plumbing emergency.

4 Systems. If you have unique or redundant systems in place to offer customers peace of mind in purchasing your product or service, then this is your selling point.

Car dealers offer loaner cars for when a purchase ends up in their shop. Electric companies have several sources of power to rely on in case a storm damages a coal plant or a nuclear plant unexpectedly scrams (shuts down). Telecommunication companies offer redundant hosts, routers, and lines in case the primary system is overloaded. My local bank changed its business hours to better accommodate customers who work traditional nine-to-five shifts. One bakery I consulted near Philadelphia keeps a full day's supply of baked goods in huge freezers at a location separate from its ovens in case its primary location is ever rendered unusable. (Why? It provides a backup supply of goods so that customers' orders are never left unfilled.) These are all examples of unique, backup, or redundant systems, ways of doing business that can deliver a little bit more to customers.

5 Incentives. Sometimes special customers deserve special treatment. Through personal experience, I know that the old marketing axiom known as the 80/20 rule is true: 20 percent of your customers will generate 80 percent of your business. These "twenty-percenters" should get special recognition or allocation of assets above all others.

Although all customers are important and should be treated accordingly, your biggest or most long-standing customers should receive a higher level of service. The airline industry recognizes this; that's why airlines reward their frequent fliers.

I have seen incentive programs run from the creative to the mundane, from the complex to the dead simple. Either way, incentive programs generally work because customers walk away from the transaction feeling that they got just a little more than expected.

For example, I like going to Waldenbooks and receiving a 10 percent discount each time I purchase a book. My son, Matthew, on the other hand, likes to go to Borders, where employees punch out a circle on a customer card for each purchase of a children's book. He knows that when he receives ten punches, he will get a $5 gift certificate. The malls are full of eateries that provide you with a customer card, encouraging you to return because you know that after you've purchased your tenth sub or slice of pizza, a free one awaits you. Video rental stores do this, too.

Thanks to McDonald's, we have a generation of children growing up on Happy Meals. If you can feed your child and get a free toy for the same price, why would you go anywhere else? McDonald's distributed flyers through my son's school that offered him a free Happy Meal for every ten books he read. That weekend, he insisted we read ten books, so back to McDonald's we went. What parent could deny rewarding a child for reading books? That's why I call McDonald's the master of incentive programs.

So, learn from the masters. Or learn from your local bookstore or video store or dry cleaners or pizza shop. Develop an incentive program that not only brings in customers but will make you look like a corporate good citizen (as with McDonald's reading program), and you've got a winning selling point.

6 **Innovation.** You know that box that motivational speakers and management gurus insist we think outside of? That's where you're going to find your innovative ideas: outside the box. When it comes to addressing client needs, the issues that you face are inside the box, just as they are for the big businesses. In fact, in-the-box issues tend to be very similar, whatever the size of a company. When big businesses are trying to solve their problems in a standardized, procedural, policy-driven, that's-the-way-we've-always-done-it way, small businesses can use creativity to come up with way-out solutions. You can think and act like a revolutionary when you are not weighted down like a corporate

dinosaur with its multiple staff levels and burdensome forms of checks and balances.

For his sixth birthday, my son wanted a model airplane powered by an air pump. "Another long list of instructions on how to put it together and fly it," I thought as I reached past it for a different item on the store shelf. Suddenly, the words "video instructions" on the air-pump-powered model plane caught my eye. "Now that's innovative," I thought. I'd seen videotapes packaged with exercise equipment and cars but never with children's toys. The plane landed in my shopping cart. Because this toy manufacturer, Spin Master Toys, was innovative, it was awarded with not only my purchase but those of thousands of other intrigued customers, making its model outsell similar versions made by large manufacturers like Mattel and Hasbro.

My favorite story of being innovative is that of a friend, Valerie Waters, a personal trainer who invented an alternative to the stodgy trailers with weight-lifting equipment that her customers (predominantly actors) used for staying in shape. Valerie opened the Muscle Truck Company, which provides clients with an innovative place to work out: fully equipped gyms on wheels that can travel to the customer. Besides state-of-the-art exercise equipment, the trucks even feature entertainment centers with surround sound, air-conditioning, recessed lighting, and mirrored walls.

The service sector provides loads of opportunities to be innovative because you're selling the way you do things in addition to the delivery of information, the work, or the accommodations.

7 **Promotional tactics.** Promotion includes just about anything you do, once established, to woo customers to your door. These tactics can be subtle or they can be blatant, making customers unmistakably aware that you are trying to woo them.

If you want to start thinking about creative tactics, listen to your local radio station: cash for the eleventh caller, a day at a salon for the best office prank of the month, a free trip to Hawaii for finding a key hidden somewhere in town. Creativity begets creativity, and analyzing even tacky ideas that worked well for another business may help you to come up with unique tactics tailored to yours.

Promoting through paradox—operating your business in a manner different from or even opposite to what is expected—can sometimes work. I saw it happen in the town where I live, at a little shop called Flowers by Jim. The owner made national headlines in 1998 when he announced to the local paper that he would be closed on Valentine's Day because he objected to the exorbitant prices that wholesalers charged for flowers on that day. He did not like charging almost double for the same bouquet of flowers on Valentine's Day that he charged on any other day. His refusal to play the game the way other florists played it came across as a sacrifice, on his busiest day of the year, for the good of his customers. His unconventional tactic paid off, and his reputation soared in town.

I once had a muffin company approach me for advice. Sales were good and it distributed its products wholesale to only four states and reported impressive, steady growth. The company wasn't interested in expanding into more states immediately. What it wanted was to become better known in its own community and to develop a good-guy slant to its reputation. I suggested that the company add a new dimension by approaching schools and civic organizations about selling its muffins for fundraisers. The tactic worked so well that the fundraising program took the company into new states even before its winning marketing strategies did.

Tactics don't have to be this involved, however; simple ones draw attention, too. For example, let's say that you hold an annual spring promotion just like all your competitors do. To distinguish yours from everyone else's, do something original like distributing your sales flyer folded around a pack of seeds. Or give away tickets to the first 100 customers for a chance to win a free spring window cleaning.

8 **Customer service.** Let's think like customers for a moment. Let's say that every card shop in your town is the same—in other words, everything from selection to quality to good location to price to incentive discounts to advertis-

ing techniques is equal. How would you decide which shop to patronize? More than likely, your decision would be based on how you feel when you shop at each location, and you'll select the one that makes you feel more welcome and more valued. But what does that mean? If you like browsing without being bothered, you will select the shop that leaves you alone. If you want immediate assistance, you will select the shop that starts helping you the moment you walk in the door.

I helped a card shop in my town turn its just-one-of-many status into an image as the most service-oriented card shop in town, with sales increasing by almost 30 percent in five months. Now, when customers walk in the door, they are greeted with a friendly hello, then told that assistance is available if they want it but that otherwise they'll be left alone to browse. Customers so inclined can describe any kind of situation for which they're seeking a card, and employees have suggestions ready. There is a play area for children so that parents don't feel rushed in making selections, and that play area just happens to make available the paints, stampers, and card stock necessary for children to make their own cards. Selecting cards sometimes takes patrons quite a bit of time, so I encouraged the shop to install coatracks to hold coats, purses, and packages. In summer, a glass of iced tea is always available, free of charge, and in winter a cup of hot chocolate puts customers in the buying mood. As customers check out, the employees always take note of whether the clients are juggling other bags, and if so, the employees provide huge shopping bags with handles to hold all the other bags. What a difference a little focus on customers made for this business.

9 **Stability and leadership.** I have not come across many small businesses that can market this feature to advantage, principally because—for most small businesses—it is not yet a strength. Sadly, this unique selling proposition is one that your largest competitors have going for them.

What I have come across are many small businesses that *thought* they should be able to rely on this selling point because they had been around for twenty years or more—

operations like office supply shops and hardware stores. Unfortunately, however, their long-standing status in town was generally not enough to help them compete with large chains like Staples, Office Max, Lowes, and Home Depot. They quickly learned that they needed to tap into (or develop) another unique selling proposition.

However, this just might be your niche, so take a look at what I mean by stability and leadership. Customers like to buy from companies that they know will be around tomorrow. They like constancy and consistency of products and services. Ask yourself:

◆ How healthy is your organization?
◆ How well capitalized is it?
◆ How long have you been in business?
◆ Are you steadfast in presentation, product, and price?
◆ Is your leadership consistent and strong?
◆ How much assurance will a customer have that you will be in business one month or one year from today?
◆ Do you have a low rate of employee turnover?
◆ Will you be able to follow through on all claims?

If the answers look positive, you may have identified a unique selling proposition that you should start promoting.

If you're still unsure where to concentrate your marketing efforts, then ask yourself these questions. The answers will help you identify your uniqueness:

◆ What do friends and family always say about you (positive comments only, please)?
◆ What are your customers saying to you about your business? (If nothing, then ask them: what's good, what's missing, what sets you apart from the others, what they would like to see?)
◆ Do you have a hobby or previous career that can support some features that could be folded into your business?
◆ What are some things you've always wanted to do in business but never had the chance?
◆ What is your marketplace lacking that you can provide?
◆ What types of people do you work with best?

Target the Right Audience

ANOTHER FACTOR IN TARGETING YOUR UNIQUE FEATURE(S) and marketing accordingly is to identify the appropriate audience of potential customers. Just as in personal relationships, you can't be everything to everybody in business either. Instead, you have to position yourself with a certain market and align every presentation effort with that market's traits, needs, and buying habits. For example, if your unique selling proposition is that you provide home delivery, then you may want to target senior citizens, whose ability to access transportation might be more limited.

Your market must have a need for what you're selling, be large enough to be considered a market segment, and be easy to reach through marketing efforts. To work as a potential market for you, its participants must be unserved, underserved, or noticeably making changes as a group in reaction to societal, physical, political, or economic situations.

I once had a client who advertised "rock-bottom" prices on clothing. In the same ad, however, he touted his large selection of exclusive designer merchandise. Thinking that he had hit upon a winning strategy by appealing to everyone, the client was surprised when the ad failed to increase sales. As I explained to him, customers do not believe that they will get both advantages in the same shop. His ad was inconsistent and made potential customers hesitate. He actually limited his buying audience to curiosity seekers. The rest of the buying public wasn't sure if the shop was a sportswear outlet, a jeans shop for teenagers, or a trendy boutique.

Once you have identified your unique selling point(s) and your target market, position your company with a strategy that encompasses every aspect of your business: displays, facility, advertising, merchandising, sales promotions, and special events.

Studies have proved repeatedly that it is less expensive to serve existing clients than it is to market to new ones. Thus if you already have a solid client base, don't be so eager to make changes that you stop maintaining the level of service that you provided when you first got these customers. If you innovate, be sure to bring customers along on your changes so they'll continue to feel special and perceive that you are serving them.

CAPITALIZE ON THE INTERNET

TAKING ADVANTAGE OF THE INTERNET TO EQUALIZE THE COMPETITION'S HEAD START

THE DYNAMICS OF THE INTERNET AND WHAT IT CAN DO FOR small businesses is a risky topic for an author to include in a book that she expects will have a long shelf life. The technology is still so unstable that we will not see long-term patterns of usage for businesses for several years.

Nevertheless, the Internet merits discussion in this book due to the potential it offers small businesses *today* to compete with larger organizations. If you can accept the mercurial temperament of the technology, spot trends, and capitalize on what you learn through your involvement on the Web, you will fare better than the average business that sets up a site simply because of pressure to do what others are doing.

Here are some reasons to evaluate the Internet as a serious medium for promoting your business:

◆ It is being viewed as the future of commerce; thus, if you have to answer "no" when someone asks if you have a Web site, you may be perceived as stuck in the past, a company that may not be around tomorrow.

◆ It is highly targeted. For example, if you sell a product that is used only by people who travel long distances in hot air balloons, you can try to draw a targeted audience to your site and place promotional material on sites that cater to hot air balloonists.

◆ It offers specialized advertising and the ability to measure ad effectiveness. Whereas the results of TV, radio, and newspaper advertising are hard to track, the Internet offers more precision. Web sites can log how many hits you receive and where these hits come from.

- It offers interactivity. You can answer visitors' questions, hold chats with them, get to know one another. Visitors can ask questions about your product or service without leaving their homes or offices.
- Given its potential to reach a vast audience of potential buyers, it is a very inexpensive promotional tool.

Study the Trends

LET'S TAKE A LOOK AT SOME OF THE TRENDS IN INTERNET TECHnology and determine how these can help you compete with more well-established competitors:

TREND ONE: CONSUMERS USE THE INTERNET FOR INFORMATION

ALL BUSINESSES SHOULD PROVIDE INFORMATION ON THE Internet, even if they are local operations. Although it's true that an attorney can't try a case on the Web (yet) and a landscape service can't rescue your weed-infested lawn online (although before long it will be able to graphically walk you through the process live), both professionals can use the Web to get you to make appointments with them by informing you of their expertise.

For a unique example of a Web site that delivers more to the visitor than what it asks for in return, check out www.theplumber.com. If this site can make plumbing interesting, you should be able to do wonders with your topic. What the founder of this site, Hill Daughtry, has done is more than build a gathering place for companies in the plumbing trade; he has also provided extensive background information on the history of plumbing and articles related to the latest practices in plumbing. He's even provided a place for visitors to find their own answers. Although Hill told me he only spends about three hours per week maintaining the site, he averages about 49,000 hits per year.

Having a Web site has become much like having a logo or a telephone listing in the yellow pages. Web sites are a must for any small business that hopes to compete with bigger, older, and better-known companies.

Any small business? Really? If you operate a gift shop in your hometown and sell principally to local customers, do you need a Web site? Perhaps not if you're the *only* gift shop in town. If you have even one competitor, however, the dynamics change. Whereas people once might have taken the time to browse both shops and read ads from both businesses, they will now—if provided with a site address—also look them up on the Internet to learn which of the two businesses best satisfies their wants.

Thus, whereas other business specialists might advise you to set up a Web site so that you can market and make more money, I say that the number-one reason to set up a Web site is so that you can first *educate* consumers, because more and more people are learning to turn to the Internet to check out a place before they commit. The Web gives visitors the opportunity to assess your abilities to do or provide what they need from a nonthreatening location (the convenience of their homes) and without fear of being taken in or coerced into buying.

Don't view your goals for a Web site as just getting more exposure, more sales, and more attention. Instead, you have to look at it as a smart step in constructing an effective educational program about your company and your products or services, an educational program that customers will be able to access twenty-four hours a day.

Let's look at two scenarios. In these scenarios, let's say that you run your own insurance agency.

In scenario one, a consumer looks up your competition on the Web. There he finds a list of all the types of insurance he might need along with their prices, neatly broken down into different options. Then he reads a rosy sales pitch about the company and the outstanding list of community services its owner has provided.

In scenario two, that consumer goes to your site. There he also finds a list of all the types of insurance he might need, but beside it are ten tips on how to cut insurance costs, along with details on a free seminar you're offering on estate planning for families. Yet another list provides him with quotes from happy customers sharing useful information (insights that solved problems) they received from your company that might benefit other consumers.

Other things being equal (such as colors, graphics, and navigability), of course the consumer will receive the more positive impression from your company, the one willing to educate him about something of interest. Neither site solicited sales of products or services online. Both merely wanted to create awareness of their services to build foot traffic to their agencies in town. The one that offers the most valuable information wins.

TREND TWO: CONSUMERS USE THE WEB TO SAVE TIME

CONSUMERS ARE BUSY PEOPLE. WE REACT TO DEADLINES, PRES-sures, and haste by collecting toys and adopting routines that will help us get it all done. Thus consumers, though busy, still want to buy and own things, and want to find services that will help them accomplish tasks and goals. The Internet provides the ability to do just that by offering a quick way to make travel arrangements, do research, contact friends, take classes, and shop.

The December 4, 1998, issue of the *San Jose Mercury News* reported that according to a survey of more than 1,000 people in the United States, "two-thirds of Internet users would rather give up their phone and TV access than Internet access." The survey, conducted by Roper Starch Worldwide, found that "three-quarters of Internet users log on regularly to make decisions on various purchases. Seventy percent said they go online to get additional information on a given product." Why? Because it educates them (trend one), and it saves them time (trend two).

TREND THREE: CONSUMERS USE THE WEB TO MAKE SHOPPING EASIER

ACCORDING TO *ENTREPRENEUR* MAGAZINE (FEBRUARY 1999) the "average online expenditure by individual Internet buyers was $227 in 1998 and is projected to be $427 in 2002." The magazine also quotes eMarketer (at www.emarketer. com, a New York firm that objectively aggregates information relating to the Internet) as reporting that consumer purchases over the Internet will "rise from $4.5 billion in 1998 to $35.3 billion by 2002."

In my research, I've learned that the main reason people buy on the Web is that they can't find the product conveniently in their immediate world. Price is not as critical a factor if the product is hard to find.

This shopping trend can benefit you if you sell products on the Web. You will not be bogged down like the large traditional businesses are, both physically and financially, with floor inventories, storefronts at prime real estate locations, and expensive insurance. You will be able to access and ship from a large inventory that resides somewhere else.

TREND FOUR: CONSUMERS ACCEPT "ALL THINGS BEING EQUAL"

WHEN JOE CUSTOMER GOES SHOPPING FOR AN ITEM IN THE nonvirtual world, he may be influenced by where the store is located, whether it's built of brick and glass or badly peeling painted wood, whether the decor puts him in the buying mood, and how friendly the staff is.

When Joe Customer turns to the Internet, however, he faces a world in which locations are rather similar. Most Web sites contain carefully crafted words, brilliant colors designed to entice the visitor to mark it as a favorite place, perhaps state-of-the-art graphics, and more and more, quality music and sound effects. The good news for small businesses is that having such a "virtual storefront" is relatively inexpensive, compared with the more traditional store. You may be able to afford a site that strongly competes with your most impressive traditional competitors because consumers see your site and theirs as being able to provide the same quality.

There still is hesitation on the part of the consumer to trust the privacy of interactions on the Internet. However, and ironically, that trust is not manifested as much in choosing a place to spend money as it is in whether to spend money at all. For example, when it comes to giving out a credit card number online, consumers are apparently as leery about giving the Amazon.coms their number as they are Big Bob's Best Books in Topeka, Kansas. (Learn from Amazon: this megasite makes customers feel comfortable spending money with them because they also welcome checks and encourage customers to place orders via their toll-free number.)

One of my favorite stories about competing with larger companies comes from Jay Massey of Coco Design Associates in Pensacola, Florida: "I was on a plane heading to Chicago for the second annual At-Home Dads Convention. Due to delays and switching planes, I ended up sitting next to a businessman who was flying back to Chicago from Atlanta. He worked for one of the largest marketing agencies in the world, and he was returning from a meeting with Coca-Cola. He said that Coke was going to be too difficult to work with and that his firm was going to decline the business. Here I was, barely six months in the black with my company, and his firm was turning down jobs of a lifetime. I told him about my company. We realized that his firm was the epitome of ultrahigh infrastructure and my company was the opposite, with no infrastructure other than that of telecommunications technology. We assumed that our respective clients also occupied opposite ends of the spectrum, until we started discussing Web design. I then found out that his company had to break out [create] small free-running design shops. . . [in order to be] streamlined enough to compete at high-tech Web design. We both realized that a particular Web job in Amsterdam that I had recently bid could well have had a competing bid from his company. I got off the plane that day feeling very good about my company and its ability to compete with larger organizations."

TREND FIVE: BUSINESSES ACTIVELY SEEK OTHER BUSINESSES ON THE WEB

IF YOU ARE A WHOLESALER OR IF YOU OTHERWISE SERVICE other businesses, then the Web is for you. Businesses have become adept at doing research and searches on the Web to find one another. In fact, according to eMarketer, business-to-business transactions will account for nearly 88 percent of all Internet dollar transactions over the next three years.

Artist Pat Merenko Smith, who founded Revelation Productions, says that the Web is a main vehicle for providing illustrated interpretations of the biblical book of Revelation to sixteen countries. "Once or twice a week I search the Web for sites that deal with Bible prophecy, and I send the owner a personal e-mail offering the free use of one of my illustrations on their Web site in exchange for a link to mine. In the first five months that we had a Web site, I got over thirty links to my site that way. It has resulted in thousands of hits and orders."

Getting Maximum Exposure for Minimum Effort

YOU DON'T HAVE TO SINK A FORTUNE INTO A WEB SITE IN order to look like a Goliath. However, you do have to have certain features if you want to go toe-to-toe with your competitors. With more than 100 million Web pages filling up the Internet, chances are you will have more competitors online than you do in the nonvirtual world. I would do you a disservice if I did not mention this: it's imperative to register with each search engine, directory, and review site. They all have pages where you can submit your URL. You can find the major ones at Poor Richard's Web Site at http://www. poorrichard.com/links/index.html#583. Note that search engine information is accessed by words or phrases, whereas indexes use subjects and categories.

◆ **Get your own domain name.** Although free Web space is offered by a number of respected services, I encourage you to avoid them, because your Web-site address—your URL, in Internet parlance—will include the name of the service. You'll appear more financially successful if you don't conspicuously use a free site.

◆ **Choose an easily remembered name.** In Chapter 1, I pointed out how limiting a descriptive name can be in traditional business interactions. On the Internet, it's the reverse. Your best bet is to establish a descriptive name so that it is easy to remember. For example, I am copresident of a company called Write Directions; our domain name is WriteDirections.com.

♦ **Include the basics on your first page.** Present your storefront in a logical and well-planned manner so that visitors' thoughts are centered on what you offer, not on making sense of your site. On your home page, carry your company's name and location, a brief statement explaining what you do and what benefits your site offers, a copyright notice, subheadings, and a table of contents with links to descriptions of products or services. Be sure to provide an e-mail response form.

♦ **Talk to a visitor's self-interest.** Wow visitors with a brief explanatory statement. Use the word "you" often. Some of the most effective sites I've seen have started out with these words: "From this site, you will. . ." and "Here you will find. . . ." In other words, readers get a sense that they will receive free information to solve a problem or to make them feel better, smarter, richer.

♦ **Include your address and phone number(s).** Even though you may be solely Internet-based, include your address and phone number. I can't tell you the number of sites I have visited while writing this book, hoping to find a means by which to contact the company in person without paying directory assistance to receive the number, only to find that these companies didn't have enough foresight to include options for getting in touch.

♦ **Add a date.** Be sure to include the date of your last update (and keep it current!) and an idea of what may be coming in the future to encourage people to visit again.

♦ **Use traditional marketing methods, too.** Just as with the traditional marketing material discussed elsewhere in this book, you should include pictures of products, catalog page layouts if you have them, testimonials from satisfied customers, and descriptions of benefits to the customer and insights into what it's like to deal with your company.

♦ **Keep your site clean and logical.** Bells and whistles and colors and graphics may make it take longer to load your pages. The more pictures you use, the more patience your potential customers will need. If images are important, use a thumbnail image that, when clicked, will link to a larger image.

◆ **Offer something free.** Visitors love getting something for nothing. Offer a free sample, brochure, report, tape, booklet, graphic, training course, membership, or consulting. For example, at WriteDirections.com we offer teleclasses in every aspect of writing. Participants can learn how to write advertising copy, a novel, a marketing brochure, a nonfiction book, a personal essay, a press release, or whatever is their interest, all by picking up the phone and participating in a combination phone and Internet distance learning class. To make them feel comfortable first and to establish trust so they know their money will be well spent, we offer free classes on several topics. Why merely describe when you can demonstrate?

◆ **Provide answers.** Offer a FAQ (frequently asked questions) page to answer the most often asked questions about your product or service.

◆ **Make it easy to order.** Make sure it's easy for visitors to find your order page and the number to call to place orders. For people who don't like giving credit card numbers over the Internet, make it easy to place orders in other ways.

◆ **Create an e-mail newsletter.** E-newsletters can offer free and educational information about your product or service, just as a traditional hard-copy newsletter does. Submit it to newsletter directory sites and offer to put visitors to your site on your mailing list.

◆ **Create a signature.** Also known as a slug line, a signature is an electronic business card that appears at the end of every e-mail message you send. It should contain all the information your business card carries: name, address, e-mail address, phone numbers, and a tag line or mission statement.

◆ **Keep studying the competition.** Web sites get better and better. Spend at least an hour per week searching for sites related to your line of work. Stay competitive!

MARKET ON A SHOESTRING BUDGET

FINE-TUNING YOUR NO- TO LOW-COST PROMOTIONAL OPTIONS

IF YOU HAVE A HUGE NEED FOR PUBLICITY AND A TINY BUDGET with which to pursue it, this section is for you. A Madison Avenue-sized advertising war chest isn't necessary. This section outlines five low-to-no-cost strategies to help you promote your company, ideas that take little more than ingenuity, elbow grease, and the willingness to fine-tune some abilities you already have and to empathize with your customers:

1 Writing
2 Speaking
3 Testimonials
4 Sponsorships
5 Free offers

First: A Word of Comfort

CAN WRITING, TALKING, AND PRACTICING EMPATHY REALLY build your business in this age of electronic communication and glitzy advertising campaigns? Yes, they can. The desire for individual attention, personal referrals, and recommendations is stronger than it's ever been. Subtle efforts like relationship marketing, networking, and word-of-mouth promotion are effective techniques for competing with your bigger and older competition.

You may think impressive advertising is necessary because you've been conditioned by its prevalence in our Goliath society. To find out how many advertisements the average consumer is exposed to regularly, I researched publications, Web sites, universities, and industry organizations and got answers as diverse as consumers are exposed to 577 advertisements each week, or they are targeted by some 2,000 each day. We have so many advertisements thrown at us from radio, television, mail, magazines, newspapers, billboards, and more that we have become skilled at hitting the mute button. Would you be able to sit down and make a list of 577 different advertisements you've encountered in the past week? Of course not. But I bet you could list the times you've experienced exceptional customer service, learned something useful from a vendor, received follow-up calls, or been asked for your opinions as a consumer. The subtle approach, the soft approach, the non-advertising approach may work best for you and your business, given your limited budget.

Second: A Word of Caution

CONSERVING ADVERTISING DOLLARS DOESN'T MEAN YOU SIT back and relax. I recommend spending a minimum of 75 percent of your marketing time and money on nonadvertising activities to build your image, reputation, reliability, and familiarity with customers. Time spent giving talks, writing articles and newsletters, participating in professional and trade organizations, making contacts, and getting and using testimonials is the most productive marketing you can do.

The difference between advertising and the subtle but deliberate efforts described in this chapter is like the difference between a Farmer and a Hunter. The Farmer plants seeds, tends them with care, and makes sure they are nurtured, all without immediate payback. He knows that if he sows and cultivates carefully, his reward eventually will be a bountiful harvest. The Hunter, on the other hand, begins each day anew seeking food. He wanders, trying to target the best place to hit big. If he has misjudged, gotten a late start, or hunted in the wrong place, he could easily go home with nothing. Subtle relationship marketing, networking, and word-of-mouth promotion are in line with the efforts of the Farmer, whereas advertising describes the Hunter.

Finally: A Word of Advice

TO THE FULLEST EXTENT POSSIBLE, USE STORIES TO TELL YOUR . . . well, story. They work for several reasons:

1 Stories are easily remembered. Hearing how a newly

designed flashlight can spot things up to 100 feet away is not as interesting as hearing how that same flashlight was used to find a missing child at 2 A.M., and that if it hadn't been for the length of the flashlight's beam, that child would have been missed in the dense woods.

2 Stories are easier to understand than descriptions, especially in the realm of technological products and services. Telling me that a software program offers full customization features, drag-and-drop interface, and 200 artist-designed templates is good. But first capture my attention with a story of how one customer used the program to create a four-page color brochure in two hours, boosting her sales by 50 percent within 48 hours of the brochure hitting the street, and then winning an award in graphic design.

3 Stories build familiarity and trust. People feel closer to the company that shares a story, because stories put otherwise dry, rote information into an emotional context.

Take, for example, a pair of hiking boots. You could expound on the details of the leather, the thickness of the soles, the comfortable elastic panels, and the smooth knit lining. It all may seem enticing information, but it is easily forgotten. Instead, tell the story of how a weary hiker was saved from a poisonous snakebite by his boots because the snake could not penetrate the thick leather, and you have a colorful story that will be remembered and associated with your product each time a consumer shops for boots.

4 Stories are a clever way to describe the benefits of a product rather than its features. Anybody who heard the last story about the hiking boots would agree that thick leather was a benefit to the wearer.

Now, let's take a look at those five no- to low-cost ideas for promoting your business.

Writing

YOU DON'T HAVE TO BE A GREAT WRITER TO PUT TOGETHER marketing pieces that can sell your business. (See Chapter 3 for more on developing your writing skills.) Nor do you have to limit your promotional writing to the standard marketing brochure. Effective marketing information that reaches customers can take many forms, including direct mail, articles, newsletters, columns, and books.

USE DIRECT MAIL

attack approach. Just don't think of it as junk mail. That's not what you are going to produce. A piece of mail is junk only if it offers nothing but a sales pitch to the recipient. Your writing and your mailings should provide value.

Direct mail can be created in many impressive and professional forms:

◆ **Personal letters.** When you mail clients an extra note, it results in their thinking about you, even feeling indebted to you, and often produces direct business or referrals. Writing letters is especially effective if you deal with a few important customers. In that situation, you should go out of your way to be personal. Send a letter to 100 past customers, prospects, colleagues, suppliers, professional contacts, friends, and other people in the community who can help spread the word. Make it unique and personal, and remind them of your product or service. For customers' letters, remind them of your other services; after all, the best prospects for your services are existing clients. For others, include an incentive to promote you or buy from you— a coupon or certificate—so that your mail is not considered junk.

If you send out mass mailings, weed through your list carefully to make sure information is correct and letters are sent only to appropriate recipients. Recently, one of my clients explained why he fired the advertising and public relations firm he had been working with: "I had dealt with the company for years. I always felt their advice was sound. I'd even had lunch with the president of the firm several times and referred other prospects to them. In spite of our long relationship, I got a letter from them addressing me as 'Ms.' The letter invited me to become a new client through a free initial consultation. I was mildly offended and wondered how much they valued—or were even aware of—my business. I figured that if they don't practice good writing and marketing, then how can they do it for me?"

◆ **Reprints from magazines.** Find relevant reprints of articles and secure permission to photocopy and distribute them. Most major companies do this.

◆ **Useful gifts.** Check out your local specialty advertising company for gifts that might be tied to your business.

◆ **Thank-you notes.** We all enjoy—and remember!—receiving a sincere thank-you, especially if it's handwritten and personally signed.

◆ **Postcards.** Use them to announce location or other business changes, expansion in your line of products or services, or upcoming specials or events.

◆ **Newsletters.** The good news about newsletters is that they are a very effective way to inform, educate, and provide timely information to customers and prospects. They are a mechanism through which you can subtly communicate about awards, honors, presentations, classes, new customers, and research results.

The bad news is that newsletters require commitment and consistency, and they can eat more of your budget than you might wish. Rather than produce expensive newsletters, try less expensive one-sheeters. Newsletters are nice, but— after time spent crafting, writing, and printing—they generally are ready to hand out right after your company has shifted focus or services. A freshly designed one-sheeter, printed on a plain, white glossy paper (with photos or not), can be folded and put into an envelope and mailed, inserted into your current brochure as an update, or given out by itself. Hand it out at trade shows and workshops, and send it by e-mail.

WRITE FOR PUBLICATIONS

DESPITE THE RUMORS OF THE DOMINANCE OF TELEVISION and the Internet over the printed word, newspapers are thriving in more than 1,600 American cities. In addition, there are more than 8,000 weekly papers and more than 6,000 consumer, trade, and business magazines published in the United States.

Articles, news releases, fillers, features, and editorials in these publications can promote and publicize you and your business. Indeed, they do the good things paid advertising is supposed to do, and they can be more effective. Coverage in a news story is more subtle than advertising but can cost less to obtain and can have more impact. News stories suggest to readers that you're at the forefront of your profession—alongside or ahead of your larger competition—whereas advertisements merely say that you have money to burn and have found a means by which to talk about yourself.

◆ **Articles.** Write articles for a trade publication or the local paper, whichever reaches your target audience. If you don't get paid for it, you can probably negotiate a byline that includes your company name, address, and service or product.

When I was heavily involved in crisis management consulting, I conducted training seminars through the Risk and Insurance Management Society. The largest class I ever taught was the one held right after I placed an article in the society's publication.

Likewise, my friend Jim Morrison, a professional speaker, sent several articles to *Master Salesmanship* magazine. After one was published, he received several calls and letters about the article and booked a few dates as a result. He then used the published article in his marketing package. He also submitted copies of the article to other magazines to request they also publish him. They did. And the process kept growing.

Besides articles, you can submit other items to publications that may get used. Share your thoughts on what important people in your field are saying, interpret industry changes or legislation, write a letter to the editor, describe the "other side of the story" in response to someone else's article, or report on polls and surveys that you conduct. Although none of these efforts may land your piece in print, they will make editors familiar with you and, over time, may prompt them to refer to you as a subject expert, a status your larger competition may not have.

Getting an article in print isn't the only reason to undertake the endeavor. The mere process of writing can be bene-

ficial to you, if you are clever about it. For example, if you
have any prospects that don't seem to take you seriously or
that remain loyal to your competition, or you don't know
how to approach them other than through a cold call, phone
them and schedule an interview for the article you are writing. During your interview, you can't help sharing what you
do professionally. This may serve you well in the future,
since business is usually given to people whom one has met
professionally.

◆ **News releases.** Write a news release every time you launch
a new program, offer new products, set new hours, hire a
key employee, change your policies, host an event, or give
out an award. The idea is to send out news releases consistently and regularly.

Remember, a release must be filled with useful information, not advertising. If you can tie your writing to something
timely, editors will like you all that much more. Look at
Chase's Annual Events Calendar at the reference desk of your
local library; it can provide many chances for a business to
create innovative and effective promotions.

Finally, include a photo, if possible, when you send a
press release. If it's a good-quality and informative photo,
your chances of getting published increase.

◆ **Columns.** Write a column. Talk to your local paper or the
applicable trade publication. Offer to write a column for free
and promise not to promote your business. You won't need
to; your byline and your expertise will build your reputation
as knowledgeable, trustworthy, and professional.

WRITE A BOOK OR BOOKLET

WRITING A BOOK OR BOOKLET CAN GREATLY ENHANCE YOUR
credibility. Publication says not only that you are an expert in
your field but that you are organized and diligent enough to
produce a major project. And if you're not, well, there is still
hope. You can hire a ghostwriter to assist you. I have served
as a collaborator to busy executives on several business
books and projects that became valuable calling cards for
them. A publication also suggests something of size behind
it, whether it's extensive expertise or a large company.

Fortunately, self-publishing and distribution is very easy these days, so if traditional publishers are not interested in your work, try alternate routes. Do have a professional writer or editor review your work before self-publishing.

Speaking

SPEAK UP. SPEAK OUT—WHEREVER AND WHENEVER YOU CAN. Speaking can make your name and message as familiar to customers as the name of your biggest competitor. Talk to every civic, business, and professional group and college classroom that will have you. I'm convinced that speaking— by presenting papers, training, conducting workshops, and offering classes—was the number-one technique that built my crisis management consulting firm. Ninety-five percent of my clients had heard me talk or train before taking me on as a consultant.

If you need to, start by taking an inexpensive public speaking class at your local community college, practice for perfection, then start speaking. But start small. This way you can gauge your effectiveness and tweak your performance in a low-risk situation. Then move on to bigger engagements at trade shows, conventions, and other gatherings where your prospects will be.

When you speak to a group, don't make it obvious that you are trying to market yourself. Instead, come across as having the attendees' best interest in mind and wanting to provide them something of value. Don't set out your marketing material. Instead, offer them something else they can take with them (see "The Free Offer," page 209). During your talk and then again when you close, mention a valuable informational piece you would be happy to send them if they leave their business card. Then you will be able to follow up personally and add their names to your data bank.

Earlier I mentioned my friend Jim Morrison, who is a professional motivational speaker based in Green Bay. Jim, who also helps people develop their public speaking skills, says, "If you know your subject well and make it interesting for the audience, public speaking is a springboard for establishing your credentials, getting recognized, and promoting your expertise and products. It establishes your business and sets you apart as an expert. It may even result in an additional revenue stream."

TEACH CLASSES

TEACH A COURSE IN THE EVENING AT A LOCAL COMMUNITY college, at your place of business, or wherever your customers might frequent. Not only might you reach prospective customers, but you also will be able to reference the experience later at opportune times. Someday when a prospect asks about your area of experience, you will be able to say with satisfaction that not only do you know it, you teach it! You may be able to drop the names of a few impressive companies into the conversation too.

Classes are a particularly effective promotional technique for people who sell services, such as real estate agents, lawyers, accountants, physicians, therapists, and sports trainers. However, almost every professional has enough knowledge to conduct a class for the consumer:

◆ A florist can demonstrate how to arrange wildflowers or make napkin rings with dried flowers.

◆ An accountant can offer a seminar discussing how to cut costs at tax time.

◆ A custom golf club maker can demonstrate how to select the perfect golf clubs at a sports club or golf range.

◆ An interior decorator can present a seminar in colors, fabrics, and furniture selection.

◆ A gift shop owner can demonstrate the top twenty ways to wrap, decorate, and deliver a present.

Testimonials

IF THERE'S ONE PERSON OUT THERE WHO LOVES YOUR PRODUCT or service and is willing to be quoted, you have not only a valued customer but also a powerful testimonial to use in your marketing efforts. Testimonials are valuable proof to prospective customers that others have used your product or service and were so satisfied that they're willing to talk about it. Testimonials suggest that you are sizable, offer a track record of success, and deliver on the promised benefits. Of all the promotional pieces I've ever written or helped clients write, the ones that include testimonials always get the most positive results. I have periodically sought testimonials from my own customers for use in promoting my services and have never been turned down or disappointed in what clients have said.

Testimonials supply the human factor that descriptions and performance claims cannot. Testimonials are particularly good for helping to explain new or misunderstood products or services. Recently a client came to me wanting help in producing a brochure. Her headline said that she "coaches women who feel overwhelmed." My first thought was that her words were too vague, because they describe every woman I've ever met. My second thought was that personal coaching is still a relatively new profession and that she should entice prospects with the benefits before she tells them where to find coaching. The most impressive way for her to do that was through testimonials.

You may have a file of letters that arrived unsolicited, thanking you for good service or describing how your product has changed someone's life. If you don't have any such letters, then you may need to solicit them. If you've done your work well or pride yourself in your product, getting such feedback shouldn't be hard. A good way to practice your business is to work not only to earn the compensation you receive, but work even harder to earn a testimonial, too. Make receiving a testimonial one of the goals of the assignment or sale from the start.

After you have completed transactions, send postcards to customers asking what they liked best about your product or service, and how it helped them live better lives or do their jobs better. The idea is to elicit specifics. An endorsement saying "I bought your computer software program, and it has become my favorite" won't motivate anyone else to buy it. But they might be motivated to buy if they read "I used your computer software program to organize my calendar and my life, and now I spend about one hour less each day tracking my sales activities."

For those comments you want to use in your marketing efforts, ask permission to quote the customer. Write up the quote and let the customer review it. You may find that he or she wants to tweak it so that it sounds even better. Next, have the customer sign off on what you have written. Seek permission to include the person's name, title or job function, city, and state. Omit street addresses to protect privacy. If you mailed the quote for review, be sure to include a self-addressed stamped envelope for mailing convenience.

How many testimonials should you use in your literature? Three is generally the best number, each being two to three lines long.

Sponsorship

FOR A LITTLE MONEY, YOU CAN GET YOUR NAME ON LITTLE League caps, a panel on the wall surrounding a ball field, a banner at the local arts festival or theater, or a float during the annual parade. Sponsorships are a terrific way for a small company to look big and well established.

Sponsorship can be particularly effective, because most conferences and theme events attract attendees with very specific profiles or interests. You can reach your targeted audience in one location or endeavor. When I worked as a public relations specialist for a commercial nuclear facility near Cleveland, I had a potential vendor approach me to find out how he could get his foot in the door with the company. He was in the business of supplying temporary technicians for refueling outages. I advised him to be a sponsor for the upcoming golf outing, because most of the refueling managers were on golf teams. As a result, he met the contacts he needed, proved he could fit in with the company's corporate culture, secured the opportunity to bid on the next refueling outage, and eventually won a contract, all for spending $200 to sponsor an event for a company he didn't work for yet.

Before you sign on the dotted line or part with money, however, do some research to ensure that your money will be well spent:

- ◆ **Review the event's history.** If it has been around for several years, make sure it actually attracts the number of people you've been told it will. If the event is new, learn as much as you can about the marketing efforts of the hosting organization.
- ◆ **Check references.** Talk to other sponsors. Can they verify that the attendees match the profiles you are seeking? Are the other sponsors pleased with their results and involvement in the event?
- ◆ **Be original.** Make sure you are the only sponsor offering the service or product that you provide. No sense competing with a bigger, more established company at the same event. Your efforts (and your money) might be wasted.
- ◆ **Determine "what if?"** Find out what happens to your money if the event is canceled due to bad weather.

The Free Offer

FREE OFFERS PERSONALIZE YOUR BUSINESS, DEVELOP THE public's image of you and the people behind your business name, and give potential customers a better feeling about doing business with you. Further, responses to a free offer generally broaden your prospect base. If your more established competitor believes itself to be beyond the need to offer anything for free, you may be able to seize some ground here.

A free offer can take many forms, from a sample of your product to a booklet that addresses a problem, giving potential customers guidance so that they can actually solve the problem without your help. Trust will develop. Don't be concerned that the potential customers will not need your service after reading the booklet; if they don't this time, they might next time, and besides, you're not going to give away all your knowledge, just enough so that if customers want to make extra efforts themselves, then they will be able to. Most customers are too busy to follow through solo. For example, suppose you hang wallpaper for a living. Providing consumers with some unusual tips that you have found to work for you will please them and prompt many to try the tips themselves. Like all good offers of helpful information, your booklet offers tips that are complete and self-contained. Once customers have tried the tips and realize how time-consuming and frustrating hanging wallpaper can be, they will pick up the phone to call for help. And who will they call? The company that they're familiar with, thanks to the reputation you've built through the free offer.

Don't offer to solve a problem that's too big. Customers won't believe it possible to get so much for free. Besides, you want them to turn to you for help on the big ones.

Your free offer could be an audiotape, a computer diskette, or a sample of something you sell. I've mentioned the free classes that WriteDirections.com, my virtual company, offers over the telephone and Internet. We do it to give participants a chance to test the waters, to verify that we offer substance, and to determine whether or not they can learn over the phone. With few exceptions, people who take our free classes sign up for fee teleclasses, because we've enabled them to make their own calculation that the value delivered far exceeds the fee charged. They walk away with useful tips and enhanced skills, and—as we've been told—they like the chance to share with other students without being in a threatening or inconvenient classroom setting.

Free offers shouldn't be limited to prospects. You can provide customers a quality free offer as a way of saying thank you for current business and as an enticement to call you again when the need arises. For example, an oil and lube shop could send a happy customer home with a free quart of oil, a women's clothing store could offer loyal customers an evening of color analysis and wardrobe design classes, and a lawn service could leave a customer a pack of flower seeds after each house call.

THOUGH CONSIDERED CONVENTIONAL, THE FIVE STRATEGIES outlined in this section can make a rather unconventional—and perhaps profound—impact on your business's growth, stability, and customer following. As you incorporate each strategy into your marketing plan, take precise notes of what works and what doesn't. But give it time. Don't get discouraged; remember, you're sowing seeds that will generate a bountiful harvest later, rather than stalking sales in the wrong places.

PRACTICE UNCONVENTIONAL MARKETING

TECHNIQUES THAT WILL MAKE YOU STAND OUT FROM YOUR COMPETITION

THIS SECTION PRESENTS NO- TO LOW-COST MARKETING TECHniques that are considered out of the ordinary, unconventional, or even daring. No idea should be considered off-limits if it works for you, is in line with your service or product, demonstrates sincerity, and displays honesty and good taste. You'll use your creativity to present your business in the way that works best for you. After all, you are the best marketer for your business, because you know it better than anyone else.

Try these unconventional—and sometimes counterintuitive—tactics to get you started or to get you thinking of other strategies that could boost your bottom line.

◆ **Solicit complaints.** Just because you're not getting any complaints from customers doesn't mean you're meeting their needs and expectations. They could be disappointed in your service or products but remain loyal because there's no other option available. . . yet. As soon as other options are available, they might take their business elsewhere, and you'll be left thinking, "If only I had known. . . ." So look like one of the big guys and do what they do: solicit feedback and complaints before a current customer becomes a former customer.

Customers rarely speak up, even when they have valid complaints. They view complaining as complicated, unnatural, negative, and a waste of time, since it often produces few results. Your goal should be to change all of those excuses. Since complaining isn't easy to do, make it as easy as possible.

A few years ago, a cousin asked me to talk to his friend, a bar owner on the outskirts of Philadelphia. The friend was distraught because a few loyal patrons had begun frequenting another bar. His gripe was "They never told me anything was wrong here. How am I supposed to know what they want if they don't tell me?" Together, we decided that he should launch a purposeful, fun, and creative campaign to solicit complaints. First, we developed posters and flyers with a picture of the bar's staff. Above the picture was the headline "We have a complaint!" Below that, the copy read, "Our complaint is that you don't give us your complaints. We want them so that we can serve you better. Share your gripes with us on . . ." and the date for a Complaint Night was posted. Everyone who complained got one free drink and a night of open grousing—about any topic. We held a contest for the best complaint of the evening. To gain entry that night, however, everyone had to share a dissatisfaction about the bar. The evening was such a success that the bar owner has continued soliciting complaints on a routine basis. Complaint forms are always available, and each month a complaint of the month is selected by patrons. The winner gets a picture taken and hung on a Complaint Wall of Fame. Below each picture is the person's grievance. At the top of the wall is this headline: "The fine experience you're enjoying tonight is brought to you courtesy of the owner and employees of (the bar's name) and these fine folks, too." As the bar owner will tell you, "This is our way of giving our customers ownership of 'their' bar. This feeling of ownership has really boosted loyalty."

◆ **Secure business whether or not you get paid for it.**
Starting a company is sometimes akin to graduating from college: you don't have the experience yet to land a good job, and until you get a good job, you can't get the experience necessary for a great job. Likewise with business. You may be too new to win projects with large companies, but until you do, you may not be able to reach the biggest companies.

Fortunately, you don't have to bid for, win, and carry out a huge assignment with an impressive company to be able to use its name in conversation. There are many ethical ways that you can practice name-dropping without having won a huge contract.

—Take a cheap flight to a city that a discount airline services and do a business presentation for any company you can find there that may have even a remote chance of buying from you. If it doesn't, well, you can at least say that you were there talking to the company. For example, you can tell prospective clients, "I was talking with Matthew Ellison at the Big Corporation in Chicago, and he said. . . ."

—Underbid for a small job with a large and well-known company so that when the job is finished, you can add that company's name to your corporate résumé.

—Volunteer your services or products to an impressive organization for a day or two. For example, if you provide a service, find out who your contact at the organization would be (the person who would actually hire you to do the job). Tell him that you would like the chance to work with him but that because you are new, you know that he probably would like to see you in action first, so to prove yourself, you would like to work for him for free for a day or two. Generally, I've seen this effort work out positively in time; and if it doesn't, you still can legitimately tell other companies that you worked with the individual.

◆ **Call key contacts and don't talk about business.** Devote three or four hours each month to call people who could be prospects or referrals for your business but with whom you haven't spoken for a while. Document your conversation in a notebook or on a computer software program so that when you talk to them next, you can refer to your notes and recall details of your conversations. To make it easy on your voice, don't try to contact everyone at once. Divide your list into groups. For example, call the As, Bs, and Cs in January; the Ds, Es, and Fs in February, and so on.

Don't ask for business. Make the phone call about them. Tell them something that will interest them. If you're not sure what your opening line should be, try this: Start making notes when you are with clients about any topics they love, personal holidays (promotions, birthdays, anniversaries, children's births), hobbies, or sports. Enter them into a master calendar or software contact manager. I once had a client who vacationed in Maine every fall. If I hadn't heard from him or had any assignments from him in a while, I would make it a point to contact him in early September to tell him to enjoy his annual trek to Maine. The phone call not only pleased him very much but always evolved into business, at his insistence. Other calls I have made included one to a client six months after he moved into a new home, just to ask how he liked the place; another was to ask a client if she was going to attend the annual conference that she had attended the year before and had enjoyed so much. People are always flattered by the gesture and the fact that you remembered something of interest to them. All it takes to practice this client-oriented service is a listening ear and good notes. This works especially well for service providers who deal with fewer customers.

◆ **Push for referrals.** Referrals are a terrific way to build business. People who have been referred to you come to you with a feeling of trust and familiarity already built in. However, sometimes clients forget to recommend you to others, no matter how happy they are with your business. They assume—since you wisely conducted yourself such that they would assume this—that you are extremely busy already. Thus, you will have to let your customers know that you want referrals. But how? With diplomacy and tact. Let a satisfied customer know that you benefit from and appreciate referrals: "Doug, I really appreciate your business and enjoy working with you. I would like to work with more clients like you. Do you have any business contacts who you feel could benefit from my services, too? If so, would you make a call and let them know what I've been able to do for you and your program? Or would you arrange an opportunity for us to meet together?" Such requests always worked like a charm for me. Doug, for example, referred me to three people who did the same work he did for other companies. Within six months, two of them had hired me.

◆ **Take your product to the streets.** Display your product in what might at first seem like unusual places, but which actually are places that your prospects frequent. For example, Reebok International Ltd. displays its sports merchandise in barbershops, delis, and parks in Los Angeles and New York City. The idea is to take your product where would-be customers hang out. Art galleries are especially effective at getting their wares displayed in eateries and convention centers.

◆ **Don't offer sales.** Some marketers argue that if you have sales all the time, people will soon buy only when you have sales. This will force you to continually sell your services and products at a discounted price. Diane of Nostalgic Notions near Cleveland discovered this the hard way. She used sales to draw people in to purchase her vintage accessories. It worked so well that she kept doing it, hoping to build her clientele. "All it did, however, is attract the same crowd, who only showed up whenever I had a sale," Diane recalls. "Eventually I realized I had to stop the sales and get across the point that my prices were thoughtfully assigned in the first place."

◆ **Market to customers' stresses and worries.** When I lived in New Jersey, I used to get flyers from a rental store in Philadelphia. Just before every holiday and seasonal celebration, a simple and inexpensive—yet always clever—flyer would arrive in the mail letting me know that the store was available for emergencies just in case my TV set died before the Super Bowl or a tent proved necessary thanks to rain on the Fourth of July or my pool filter didn't work for Memorial Day or I needed floodlights for Halloween. Of course, when I needed to rent a carpet cleaner and tent, I turned to them.

◆ **Market to somebody else's customers.** This advice proved beneficial for a caterer I once worked with. Although business was good, she wanted to reach new markets. Because caterers are usually associated with festive times, we developed a promotion in which she would reach people through the happiest times of their lives. She approached hospital personnel with the idea that new mothers should return to housework slowly after coming home with a new baby. As a result, they allowed her to distribute flyers offering a discounted "Welcome Home Mommy and Baby" luncheon, delivered to their home. The flyers were given to new fathers and grandparents on the day of birth. Of course, in their joy and desire to help the new mom as much as possible, many of them called immediately and scheduled a celebratory luncheon. And when the caterer delivered the luncheon, she left flyers about a special baptism celebratory luncheon she also provided. Generally, the now-satisfied customers were more than happy to book her, giving them one less thing to worry about. This wise caterer, now getting the idea of anticipating needs in advance and striking deals, approached music teachers in town and offered them a free dozen homemade pastries on the day of their choosing if, in return, they would distribute flyers to parents of music students about a "Post-recital Celebratory Gathering." Again, parents were thrilled at the idea and pleased that they knew someone who could provide such a service so that they wouldn't have to go shopping. Many hadn't even thought of hosting a gathering after the recital until they received the flyer.

◆ **Entice them into your shop.** When I was a freshman in college, I frequented a shop that specialized in dry roasted nuts of all kinds. The nuts were good, but nothing worth stopping for when, if you drove just a few more miles, you could visit a potato chip factory, get your desire for salt satisfied, and take a free tour of the factory. By my sophomore year, the owner of the nut shop had displayed about two dozen elephants of all sizes, shapes, and materials on his shelves. They were so popular that by my junior year he began hanging posters filled with statistics and information about elephants from around the world. By my senior year, he had built on to his shop, devoting at least half of the facility to an elephant museum. He bought the vacant lot across the street to provide more parking space. Media coverage followed, and he had a bona fide hit on his hands.

◆ **Create an award or honor.** Bestowing an award, such as a gift certificate, a scholarship, or even just a plaque for an area of excellence, builds goodwill and customer loyalty and suggests you have a sizable company behind you. And then, of course, there is all the free publicity you will receive during the announcement of the annual nominee search, the

announcement of the semifinalists, the presentation cere-
mony, and the news features about what the winner will do
with the award.

Besides awards, try creating honors (patron of the arts,
most honest attorney, teacher of the year), certificate programs (for completion of hours of community service,
years spent using your product), or an institute (a center or
clearinghouse for specific information) to attract attention
to your efforts as a supporter of the community. For example, public relations specialist Alan Caruba created two centers: one a media spoof, the Boring Institute; and the other
a center dedicated to media-driven scare campaigns, the
National Anxiety Center. "As a result," Caruba says, "I do
an average of 1,000 radio interviews annually that keep my
name before the public and enhance my PR reputation
with clients who hear me or see me on the occasional TV
interview. These two activities have evolved into businesses
in their own right, selling related products, guides, and
other merchandise." No one would know that Caruba's
business is home-based.

◆ **Create attention with a contest.** Holding a contest is a
great way to get name recognition and to position yourself in
the marketplace. It's also a good way to waste a lot of time
and money if the results don't pan out. Unlike an award, a
contest is generally seen as an attempt at publicity and is
sometimes ignored by news media until the actual presentation of the prize.

The best contests are those that fit into your schedule and
fill your needs, as opposed to ones that use up your time
and money by taking you away from your purpose. For
example, at the Bedford Old-Fashioned Days in Bedford,
Pennsylvania, near where I grew up, I remember a contest
hosted by a local jeweler that took little of his time yet
brought lots of visitors into his store. And once there, of
course, they would look around for a while. What he would
do is send an employee into the streets to distribute a num-
bered tag in either blue or yellow to each adult visitor to
Old-Fashioned Days. The visitors' assignment was to find
the wearer of that same number in the other color. Each tag

featured the name of his store, and of course, people wore them prominently pinned on their chests because they wanted to be spotted by their twin. Once "twins" were matched, they proceeded to the store to enter a grand-prize drawing for a diamond. The jeweler also had cookies and punch available so that visitors would linger and browse. Even as a child I knew the man had a marketing concept underway, because I witnessed these people asking to see items from his display case.

◆ **Barter for business.** If you come across someone with whom you can exchange services, favors, or business, then begin bartering. Pat Merenko Smith, artist and president of Revelation Productions, bartered her way to a successful exchange with her artwork of the biblical book of Revelation. "There are many high-profile ministries nationally that deal almost exclusively with Bible prophecy, and most of them produce full-color magazines or newsletters that they send monthly to their hundreds of thousands of supporters. Initially, several of them contacted me asking to use my art in their magazines or promotional materials," she explains. "I would quote the usual fee for use of my art, and then I would add, 'But if you will give me a promotional credit line with our phone number and Web address, I'll cut the price of using the art by 50 percent.' A couple of them even offered to do an article about me and my work, in which case I offered them the free use of three of my illustrations. This bartering has worked wonderfully, and sales are usually quite brisk after those publications are distributed, because I have a targeted audience."

◆ **Reach your customers in unexpected ways.** Employees at large companies may be bound to certain company-established codes of marketing, but you are not. My friend Ginny owns several gift boutiques in the Washington, D.C., area. Two years ago she created small but highly decorative tissue-box holders that hang on the inside of the car door—much like a hanging cup holder. Convinced because the holders had sold so well in her own shops that others might be interested in selling them in their stores, too, she attended a national gift sellers convention. Wisely, Ginny knew that the product would be just one of thousands on display and that the product stood its best chance of selling if customers could see it—even use it—in its proper environment. Thus, she got a part-time job as a taxi driver. She placed the tissue holders on each side of the backseat of the cab and by the front passenger seat. Then she started to work, picking up passengers from the convention hall only and making a point of holding conversations with them about the tissue holders. She talked to anyone who would listen; fortunately that list included quite a number of buyers. Most of the time, Ginny reports, the passengers noticed her product and made comments before she had to mention it. Her efforts brought in orders worth thousands of dollars.

◆ **Host a fund-raiser.** When the local Frederick Youth Symphony Orchestra needed to raise money to go to Spain, Uncle Ralph's Cookies stepped in, allowing its cookies to be sold as a fund-raiser for the event. As president Peggy Wight explains, the fund-raiser "started out as a test to see how well it would go. It soon took on a life of its own." The company owners were so happy with the success of the event that they wrote a press release and announced their new endeavor in local papers. That was in 1997. The next year, according to Peggy, sales from fund-raisers tripled. "It became a profitable and full-time way of promoting our products," she says. "We've even hired someone to head the fund-raising efforts."

◆ **Offer at least one feature more than the competition.** Recently, my neighbor wanted to put a wood floor in his hallway. To save money, he decided to install it himself. After shopping around for the flooring, he discovered that he would need to use a plank nailer so that he could nail the wood to the floor at an angle, thus eliminating the nail showing on the tongue of the tongue-and-groove floor. Only one store in town offered free use of a plank nailer if you purchased the wood there; not even the home supply superstores equaled this offer. Since a plank nailer would cost about $240 above the cost of the wood, my neighbor wisely bought his wood at the small business where he could use the tool for free.

◆ **Approach advertising cautiously.** Most people would agree that small businesses survive because they build a reputation for providing the personalized product or service that seems to be lacking in bigger organizations. Yet the moment those same small but successful businesses begin to grow and make money, many begin practicing conventional advertising so that they can grow bigger quicker. Thus, they hop into an arena with the big companies before they're really ready to be there. In my opinion, they produce as much financial waste and frustration as they do sales at this point. As you enter the same class as your competition, it's precisely the time when you need to be different, not more of the same. This means reaching your market personally and directly.

Why? Because customers lured by ads tend to be fickle, not loyal. Advertising doesn't necessarily provide a solid customer base or repeat sales, and you want both during your growth stages.

Advertising professional services can be especially unproductive. What proof can an ad present that you can deliver quality service? Better to shoot for testimonials in your marketing material, or develop and promote (and yes, even advertise) the availability of an information product such as a booklet, as described earlier in this section. While you're at it, consider charging a small fee for the product. A fee helps weed out those who are not serious or in need of your service.

If you are still determined that advertising suits your purposes, then take an unconventional approach: research your options well before spending money. Why is this unconventional? Because most businesses don't bother researching. Instead, they simply turn to the local paper or radio station and pay for an ad.

Each medium has a specific target audience. Each radio station, TV program, newspaper, magazine, and newsletter tries to cater to specific segments of the population. The trick is to determine what media your main customers use, then try to reach them and others like them through media. For example, besides being very costly, TV reaches a mass audience of people of varying ages and lifestyles (great for selling food, shampoo, or cards), whereas radio is highly targeted to particular audiences (good for selling products to teens or seniors, for example). Trade journals reach a very specific targeted audience, whereas newspapers touch a broader group of people, particularly home owners, business personnel, and community leaders.

HERE ARE SOME SUGGESTIONS TO HELP YOU IN YOUR RE-search of advertising media:

◆ Ask the sales department for demographics and qualitative analysis of the audience they reach. They should provide you with enough information to help you determine whether your product or service is compatible.

◆ Find media you can afford to use again and again. The key to effective advertising is consistency. Don't spend your entire advertising budget on one or two expensive ads. You have to present your message over and over. Most marketers believe that it takes at least six weeks of repetition for your advertising message to become familiar to your audience.

◆ Find out what media work for your competitors. However, don't mistake what they use with what actually works. Do some sleuthing to find out.

And finally, don't try to develop ads on your own. Seek professional help, then test the ad on friends, family, neighbors—anyone who will talk to you. Make sure it imparts the message and the reaction you are seeking.

Afterword

ning for you and your company as you ponder, adopt, test, and apply these magnifying ideas.

My goal has been to provide bottom-line value from beginning to end. So now that you're ready to close the back cover, I'd like to offer you one thing more. As the barking circus ringmaster says, I've "saved the best for last." Let me tell you about Scott Testa, president of Mindbridge.com, who has practiced the techniques in this book from 1997, when he founded his company with $15,000 in the basement of his home—complete with a yelping basset hound and a swooshing, whirling washing machine that sometimes served as a countertop—to his success today, with seventy-five employees and multimillion-dollar sales.

Testa would think I made his original office sound good. In his words, "My home is one of these older homes, with a smelly, stinky, falling-apart basement. Few and tiny windows. No natural light. Wet. Small. One step up from a dungeon, without the shackles."

And, he says, if clients had seen where he and his partner, Dave Christian, were while they designed their interactive Web sites, Mindbridge.com never would have gotten the sales.

When asked why he used the enhancements he did, Testa says, "Willie Sutton, the famous bank robber, was asked by a reporter why he robbed banks. Willie responded, 'Because that is where the money is.' In order to grow the company, we knew we had to have the image of a large company, from our business cards to our Web site to our telephone system. In essence, anything that portrayed our identity to the outside world was where we spent our money. The bottom line is that large companies like to do business with other companies that they perceive as having a presence, being large, or at least being very professional. Without this attitude, we would have never gotten out of the basement."

Testa did what clever entrepreneurs do. He didn't lie; he marketed to people's perceptions. There were many winter days when rather than let a client overhear his dog and his washing machine, he simply stepped outside into the sin-

223

gle-digit temperatures to hold a conversation on his cordless phone.

Like Testa, you need to think perception until it becomes second nature. So here, once again, are the precepts:

CRAFT THE RIGHT IMAGE

FROM THE WAY YOU DRESS TO THE NAME YOU ASSIGN YOUR company to the way you describe it, you need to develop an image that changes prospects' perceptions and wins you customer loyalty, no matter what your size or line of work. Testa was used to referring to his company as "we" instead of "I" and to meeting clients at the airport, from which he ushered them to a hotel business suite that was stocked with food, so that the clients—one being the information technology manager from General Electric—didn't request a visit to his "office." Testa adds, "We used to borrow my parents' new Lincoln instead of using our cars, which were ten years old. We also had our stationery printed with the fictitious suite number of 732. There was no suite 732, of course, but it was my house number, and the mail was still delivered without a problem."

INVOLVE OTHER PEOPLE IN YOUR PLANS

USE CONTACTS, FAMILY, OR EMPLOYEES TO YOUR ADVANTAGE while keeping them as involved or uninvolved as you want them to be. When Testa finally moved out of his basement office, he leased a space much larger than his company needed immediately. He overcame the "you're-not-busy" perception by moving all his employees into the office area that clients visited.

TURN DAILY ROUTINES INTO OPPORTUNITIES

MAKE YOUR BUSINESS PRESENTABLE BY TWEAKING DAILY mundane business rituals into promotional efforts. As I was corresponding with Testa, I noted that his e-mail account began with "STesta," rather than "Scott." Why announce that they're so small that they only have one Scott at the company?

MARKET FOR OPTIMUM IMPACT

OPTIMIZING YOUR IMAGE MEANS FINDING YOUR MARKETING niche, unifying your image in everything you do, taking advantage of the Internet, and practicing some unconventional marketing. From the start, Testa says he walked away from smaller clients to focus on the bigger ones. That cost him money at first, but in the end he was able to say that his client list included Sony, *Better Homes & Gardens,* and Houghton Mifflin.

Today, Mindbridge.com, the Fort Washington, Pennsylvania–based company, is quickly on its way to achieving the same Goliath stature as the companies with which it used to compete. At the time of this writing, Testa plans an initial public offering within a year. "Now what scares us is not only the large companies but the companies that were in our shoes two years ago—the ones in the basements and the garages. The ones who are hungry. . . who come from nowhere and have the potential to start eating our lunch." And with a smile, he adds, "The small competitors are the ones to fear."

Thanks, Scott, I couldn't have said it better.

GOOD LUCK IN YOUR EFFORTS TO OUTSMART THE GOLIATHS IN your industry. I welcome your comments, reactions, and experiences. You can e-mail me at Debra@Outsmarting-Goliath.com or write to me at P.O. Box 86, Walkersville, MD 21793.

Resources

Resources

EACH RESOURCE BELOW FEATURES A WEB LOCATION BECAUSE the Internet is a small business owner's best friend, bringing a world of information to your digital doorstep with speed, precision, and (most of the time) accuracy. During your search for information and your efforts to share information about your business, no one ever has to know how big or successful your company is. You can remain a small business, yet deliver a big-business impact.

No doubt your established competition is leveraging the power of the Internet to help them maintain their distinction as bigger, older, richer, or better known, so this resource section is designed to assist you in capitalizing on your equal access to the Internet to promote your unique selling points.

Entries generally provide an Internet address. If a site required visiting more than four pages to learn its address and phone number, then these items were not included. Chapter 4 explains why.

ACCESSIBILITY TO CUSTOMERS

IF YOU'RE NOT LISTED AT THE FOLLOWING WEB SITES, YOU MAY be missing a valuable opportunity to market. These are becoming the sites people visit to find established businesses and organizations. Imagine how unimpressed they will be if you are not listed here. To add your listing, simply visit the site and click on the appropriate selection. From there, all that is required is filling out a form.

◆ **AnyWho: www.anywho.com**
◆ **Switchboard: www.switchboard.com**
◆ **WhoWhere: www.whowhere.com**

BUSINESS ASSOCIATIONS

◆ **Better Business Bureau (www.bbb.org)**
Being a member of the Better Business Bureau (BBB) will build your credibility with prospects. After all, fly-by-night companies generally do not bother to apply. You can also find the BBB in your local telephone directory.

◆ **Census Bureau (www.census.gov)**
This site offers Subjects A-Z, a search option, a catalog, and Access Tools to click on, among others. These tools are great for helping you develop a profile of your market and for determining how extensive your competition is.

◆ **Chamber of Commerce Small Business Center (www.uschamber.org)**
202-659-6000
1615 H Street, NW
Washington, DC 20062
Get involved in the chamber of commerce near you. It looks good on your corporate résumé.

◆ **Consumer Information Center (www.pueblo.gsa.gov)**
888-8-PUEBLO (888-878-3256)
Department 91
Pueblo, CO 81009
This site offers full text versions of booklets published by the U.S. government on a variety of issues, including small business ownership. View them for free or purchase printed copies at the online ordering site.

◆ **Copyright Office (lcweb.loc.gov/copyright/)**
202-707-3000
101 Independence Avenue, SE
Washington, DC 20559
Copyright your materials to give them the look of importance.

◆ **International Association of Business Communicators (www.iabc.com)**
800-776-4222 / 415-544-4700
One Hallidie Plaza, Suite 600
San Francisco, CA 94102
Worth visiting just to review the archived articles from the association's publication, *Communication World*.

◆ **International Trademark Association (www.inta.org)**
212-768-9887
1133 Avenue of the Americas
New York, NY 10036
Learn more about filing and protecting a trademark.

◆ **National Association for the Self-Employed (www.nase.org)**
800-232-6273
P.O. Box 612067
DFW Airport
Dallas, TX 75261-2067
This association exists to serve the small business owner. What more do I need to say?

◆ **National Federation of Independent Business (www.nfibonline.com)**
615-385-9745
3322 West End Avenue, Suite 700
Nashville, TN 37203
Worth noting because this Web site discusses how government regulations have interfered with your business.

◆ **U.S. Small Business Administration (www.sbaonline.sba.gov)**
800-827-5722 / 202-205-6605
409 Third Street, SW
Washington, DC 20416
Why pay for advice on how to expand your business when you can get much of it for free, courtesy of the U.S. government? The Small Business Administration (SBA) offers step-by-step guidance in several disciplines.

BUSINESS MANAGEMENT

◆ **BizPlus (www.bizplus.com)**
This site offers loads of links for small business information, including picking a name for your company and securing trademarks. But, of course, read Chapters 1 and 3 in this book first.

◆ **EntreWorld (www.entreworld.org)**
Presented by the Kauffman Center for Entrepreneurial Leadership, this site touts itself as an online information source for entrepreneurs. It groups information by stages of business development, such as Starting Your Business, Growing Your Business, and so on. Entrepreneurs hoping to compete with Goliaths might find the listing of seminars and conferences (which is searchable by location) worthwhile for interacting with like-minded individuals.

◆ **Microsoft Smallbiz (www.microsoft.com/smallbiz)**
Microsoft never seems to disappoint, as evidenced by this site. The many feature stories and directories of small business resources will prove handy in your attempt to polish your image.

◆ **Service Corps of Retired Executives (www.score.org)**
This site has much potential. The Service Corps of Retired Executives (SCORE), a nonprofit resource partner with the Small Business Administration, is made of more than 12,000 retired executives who offer free counseling to small businesses. It has potential because, as a small business owner, you can select from a list of skills and industries to find an appropriate counselor, then you can get advice via e-mail. If you're smart, you'll establish a relationship with a counselor and turn it into a mentorship or a road to important referrals.

◆ **Small Business Knowledge Base (www.bizmove.com)**
Features practical information on topics such as marketing plans and personnel audits, so it's worth wading through the many advertisements presented there.

MARKETING TOOLS
◆ **American Demographics (www.demographics.com)**
Through online features and the *Forecast* newsletter, you can review demographic trends and business forecasts and develop a profile of your audience.

◆ **Business Profiles (www.infousa.com)**
Wonder what your competition is up to? Find information about a business, including number of employees, sales volume, key executives, lines of business, credit codes, and much more.

◆ **Mediafinder (www.oxbridge.com)**
Here you will find the lowdown on about 100,000 publications. It's great for planning a news release campaign or mailing to speciality publications in your field.

◆ **Poor Richard's Web Site**
(www.poorrichard.com/links/index.html#583)
Here you will find major search engines, directories, and review sites where you can submit your URL. Back up to the home page and, amid the loads of advertising and self-promotion, you'll find a site that offers value to the small business owner.

◆ **The Roper Center for Public Opinion Research**
(www.ropercenter.uconn.edu)

860-486-4440
University of Connecticut, U-164
Montieth Building
341 Mansfield Road, Room 421
Stoors, CT 06269
The Roper Center claims to be the largest library of public opinion data in the world. And since I couldn't find any larger, we'll assume it is. The site's tag line is clever and appropriate: "Where thinking people go to learn what people are thinking."

◆ **Write Directions (www.WriteDirections.com)**
301-694-9921
P.O. Box 1936
Frederick, MD 21702
This may be shameless self-promotion, but I think that my company's Web site is a business owner's best friend when it comes to business and personal writing. We offer distance-

learning classes in writing over the telephone, supplemented with handouts via the Internet. What could be more convenient? You'll also find a place to secure one-on-one consulting help with whatever writing or marketing project you are undertaking.

NAMING YOUR COMPANY

◆ **Internet Network Information Center (www.networksolutions.com)**
To determine whether another business is using the name that you want on the Internet, check with the Internet Network Information Center (InterNIC) domain name registration service.

◆ **Patent and Trademark Office (www.uspto.gov)**
703-308-4367
General Information Services Division
Crystal Plaza III, Suite 2C02
Washington, DC 20231
To determine whether the name that you want has been registered with the U.S. Department of Commerce's Patent and Trademark Office, go to this site.

◆ **State/Local government on the Web (www.piperinfo.com/state/states.html)**
Check a business name's availability in your state by going to the Department of State Web site for the state in which you want to establish a business. Piper Resources provides this link to state governments on the Web.

◆ **Switchboard (www.switchboard.com)**
The quick-and-dirty way to find a listing of potential names (and whether a business already has a name that you want, regardless of location) is by checking a telephone directory on the Internet. Switchboard is the one to start with.

OFFICE SUPPLIES

◆ **The Mobile Office Outfitter (www.mobilegear.com)**
800-426-3453
925-485-5630
Who could argue that a site that bills itself as the mobile office outfitter could be a small business owner's best friend? This site offers a full line of mobile office products, just the thing solo entrepreneurs or struggling business owners need to cover the fact that they must simultaneously be in the office and out and about.

◆ **Office supply stores**
These four sites are equally impressive, convenient, and stocked with supplies. Since your local office supply store could be your mainstay for marketing and presentation materials, why not save time by visiting its Web site (or calling) instead?
Office Depot: www.officedepot.com
OfficeMax: www.officemax.com
OnlineOfficeSupplies: www.onlineofficesupplies.com
Staples: www.staples.com

REFERENCE AND RESEARCH

◆ **Search engines (www.google.com and www.dogpile.com)**
These two search engines seem to check the most news wires, newsgroups, and other search engines. Google, for example, ranks every page on the Internet in order of importance, which is determined by the number of other links that point to it. Thus, the first few results listed will probably provide the answers and the reliable sources you seek.

STORAGE OR BACKUP

◆ **Backup Your Files (www.atbackup.com, www.freedrive.com, and www.atrieva.com)**
As discussed in Chapter 3, nothing shouts "small" as quickly as having to announce to a client that you lost a vital file. Visit these sites for options on backing up your hard work.

Publications

THE FOLLOWING LIST IS SELECTIVE, NOT COMPREHENSIVE.

BOOKS

◆ **Applegate, Jane.** *201 Great Ideas for Your Small Business*
(Bloomberg Press, 1998, $14.95)
The advice is great, but the book is worth buying just for the
contacts she has jammed within the text; as a well-known
syndicated business columnist, she has many of them.

◆ **Levinson, Jay Conrad.** *Guerrilla Marketing: Secrets for
Making Big Profits from Your Small Business* (Houghton Mifflin, 1998, $13)
This book, more than most in Levinson's *Guerrilla* series,
offers practical examples of marketing that deliver big results
for small businesses.

◆ **Taylor, Dan, and Jeanne Smalling Archer.** *Up Against the
Wal-Marts* (AMACOM, 1996, $14.95)
The authors detail what it takes for a small retailer to com-
pete with companies the size of Wal-Mart and Home Depot.

MAGAZINES AND JOURNALS

◆ **Business Marketing (www.crain.com)**
Crain Communications, Inc.
312-649-5200
740 Rush Street
Chicago, IL 60611
Crain Communications is primarily a publishing company
producing business, trade, and consumer newspapers and
magazines. Its specialty business publications will be of particular interest to savvy entrepreneurs.

◆ **Entrepreneur (www.entrepreneurmag.com)**
800-274-6229
2392 Morse Avenue, P.O. Box 19787
Irvine, CA 92714-9438
On the day I reviewed this site for inclusion in this book, it

had an article posted entitled "Playing with the Big Boys," about two owners of a small business who did a few magnifying tricks to make themselves appear larger than they were. Thus, I figured this site is worth visiting.

◆ **Home Business Journal (www.homebizjour.com)**
315-865-4100
9584 Main Street
Holland Patent, NY 13354
This publication doesn't look as slick as the other magazines listed here, but the information is just as helpful.

◆ **Home Office Computing and Small Business Computing (www.smalloffice.com)**
800-288-7812 / 212-505-3580
730 Broadway
New York, NY 10003
Exceptional publications that pack a lot of information between the covers. The Web site has much to offer, too.

◆ **Inc. (www.inc.com)**
617-248-8000
800-234-0999
38 Commercial Wharf
Boston, MA 02110
Both the Web site and the magazine claim to be the location for "growing companies." I agree. Turn here for information on how other formerly small companies found success.

◆ **Success Magazine (www.successmagazine.com)**
800-234-7324
P.O. Box 3038
Harlan, IA 51537
This publication gets a thumbs-up for the variety of material it covers. Also good is the Web site, which on the day I reviewed it for possible inclusion here featured a story on how customer service is the best way to reach Generation X. Since this coincides with what I say in this book, I think it's right on target.

Index

credit card(s), 58, 61
credit policies, 61
customer service, 10, 12, 70–71
   availability of, 13*t*
   complaints assigned in, 102
   educating client through, 42
   employee concern for, 100–101
   entrepreneur and, 101–102
   guidelines for, 102
   listening as, 213–214
   niche for, 180, 185–186
   specialized, 177–178

D

delivery, overnight, 165, 170–171
Dudley, Denise, 24

E

editor, 203
education, full services for client through, 42–43
electronic materials, 156–157
e-mail
   call name for, 224
   conversion of, 129–130
   information purposes of, 64
   newsletters for, 197
   retrieval of, 163
   voice messaging and, 121, 129–130
employees, 98
   business practices with, 99
   customer service from, 100–102
   family as, 90–95, 96*t*–97*t*
   hiring of, 95, 98
   image and, 90–92, 95–103
   implied staffing and, 157
   insurance for, 99
   job descriptions for, 95
   motivation for, 99–100
   negatives of, 91–92

F

separation of work for, 96t–97t
slow times in, 92
spouse and, 96t–97t
tax advantages of, 92–93
telephone and family in, 127, 129
vision of, 93
fax machine transmissions, 121–125, 159–163
flyers, 212, 215–216
forms, 156, 159–161
free offers. *See* marketing, free offers
fundraising, 219

G

Gateway, Inc., 100–101

H

Harvard University, 180
home business, 28–29, 70
honesty, 36–38

I

image
address as, 10–11, 26–29
assessment of, 14–16
company's name as, 17–26
corporate, 10
crafting of, 11, 223–225
differentiation from competition and, 12t–13t
employees and, 90–92, 95–103
factors controlling, 12t–13t
family-based business and, 90–95, 96t–97t
improvement plan for, 16–17
logistics of company and, 12t
marketing materials and, 138–144, 150–160
negativity and, 14
personal building of, 47–60
preconceptions and, 12t
safeguarding of, 60–69
scope and depth of, 13t

N

e-mail and, 197
for many clients, 144
one-sheeter as, 202
own company's, 144–145
qualities of, 202
your picture in, 144
noncompete clause, 88

O

opportunity, 16–17
outsourcing, 88–89

P

pager, 127
partner(s), 82–87
pets, 96*t*, 127, 135*t*
photo, 144, 204
Poor Richard's Web Site, 95
pricing, 12*t*, 178
prospects, 82
publications, 202–204

Q

quality, 12*t*

R

receivables, 161–162
referrals, 214
confirm, 110
awards for, 114
Rent-a-Husband Inc., 21
résumé, 11, 144
corporate, 213
Risk and Insurance Management Society, 110, 203

S

sales, 67
sales representatives, 89, 99
seminars, 119, 181

V

voice messaging (voice mail), 120–122, 128–130
Voice Response Corporation, 134–136
volunteer, 213

W

Warren, Kaile, Jr., 21
workshops, 149–150
WriteDirections.com, 40, 84, 197, 210
writing. *See* marketing, writing
writing errors, 139–140

About Bloomberg

Bloomberg L.P., founded in 1981, is a global information services, news, and media company. Headquartered in New York, the company has nine sales offices, two data centers, and eighty news bureaus worldwide.

Bloomberg Financial Markets, serving customers in 100 countries around the world, holds a unique position within the financial services industry by providing an unparalleled combination of news, information, and analytic tools in a single package known as the BLOOMBERG PROFESSIONAL™ service. Corporations, banks, money management firms, financial exchanges, insurance companies, and many other entities and organizations rely on Bloomberg as their primary source of information.

BLOOMBERG NEWS℠, founded in 1990, offers worldwide coverage of economies, companies, industries, governments, financial markets, politics, and sports. The news service is the main content provider for Bloomberg's broadcast media, which include BLOOMBERG TELEVISION®—the 24-hour cable and satellite television network available in ten languages worldwide—and BLOOMBERG® RADIO™—an international radio network anchored by flagship station BLOOMBERG® RADIO AM 1130 in New York.

In addition to the BLOOMBERG PRESS® line of books, Bloomberg publishes BLOOMBERG® Magazine, BLOOMBERG PERSONAL FINANCE™, and BLOOMBERG® WEALTH MANAGER.

About the Author

Debra Koontz Traverso has worked for, with, and around Goliaths for more than eighteen years, as a business journalist, marketing communications specialist, management consultant, and business owner. She has been a consultant to scores of small and large businesses including UPS, NASA, Dow Chemical, United Airlines, Nike, and Coopers & Lybrand. She is also an adjunct faculty member at Harvard University and copresident of WriteDirections.com, which offers consulting and distance learning classes in business and personal writing. She lives in the Washington, D.C., area. Readers may reach her at Debra@OutsmartingGoliath.com.

VINCENT J. LaSCOLA II